Bex Lockyer

W9-CMZ-717

Julius Caesar

SHAKESPEARE IN PERFORMANCE

Advisory Editors: **David Bevington and Peter Holland**

methuen | drama

First UK edition published 2007

A & C Black Publishers Limited
38 Soho Square
London W1D 3HB
www.acblack.com

© 2006 Sourcebooks Inc.
First printed in the U.S. by Sourcebooks MediaFusion

ISBN 978-0-7136-8357-8

A CIP catalogue record for this book is available from the British Library.

Cover Design by Jocelyn Lucas

Cover Illustration © Ann Elson 2007

CD manufactured by Lemon Media

Printed and bound in Great Britain by The Bath Press, Bath

To students, teachers, and lovers of Shakespeare

Contents

About Sourcebooks MediaFusion   vi

About the Text   vii

On the CD   ix

Featured Audio Productions   xiii

Note from the Series Editors   xv

In Production: *Julius Caesar* through the Years   1
    by Robert Ormsby

As Performed: By Theatre for a New Audience   13
    at the Lucille Lortel Theatre in New York City in 2003
    by Jeffrey Horowitz

"O, What a Fall Was There, My Countrymen!":   23
    Julius Caesar in Popular Culture
    by Douglas Lanier

JULIUS CAESAR BY WILLIAM SHAKESPEARE   33

The Cast Speaks: The Shakespeare Theatre of New Jersey's 2005 Cast   281
    by Marie Macaisa

A Voice Coach's Perspective on Shakespeare: 299
    Keeping Shakespeare Practical
    by Andrew Wade

In the Age of Shakespeare   307
    by Thomas Garvey

About the Online Teaching Resources   319

Acknowledgments   321

Audio Credits   323

Photo Credits   325

About the Contributors   327

ABOUT SOURCEBOOKS MEDIAFUSION

Launched with the 1998 *New York Times* bestseller
We Interrupt This Broadcast and formally founded in 2000,
Sourcebooks MediaFusion is the nation's leading publisher
of mixed-media books. This revolutionary imprint is dedicated
to creating original content—be it audio, video, CD-ROM,
or Web—that is fully integrated with the books we create.
The result, we hope, is a new, richer, eye-opening,
thrilling experience with books for our readers.
Our experiential books have become both bestsellers
and classics in their subjects, including poetry (*Poetry Speaks*),
children's books (*Poetry Speaks to Children*),
history (*We Shall Overcome*), sports (*And The Crowd Goes Wild*),
the plays of William Shakespeare, and more.
See what's new from us at www.sourcebooks.com.

About the Text

As the only authoritative early text of *Julius Caesar* is that found
in the First Folio (F1) of 1623, that edition serves as the copy-text for
this edition. Although the F1 text has been silently modernized,
any significant variations are recorded in the notes and speech prefixes
have been regularized, usually without notation. Material, particularly
stage directions, that is editorially added is enclosed in square brackets [ ].

On the CD

1. Introduction to the Sourcebooks Shakespeare *Julius Caesar*: Derek Jacobi

ACT 1, SCENE 2, LINES 2–24
2. Narration by Derek Jacobi
3. Harold Gould as Caesar, Jack Coleman as Casca, Bonnie Bedelia as Calphurnia, Richard Dreyfuss as Mark Antony, Basil Langton as Soothsayer, Stacey Keach as Brutus, John de Lancie as Cassius
   L.A. Theatre Works • 1995
4. John Moffat as Caesar, Brian Haines as Casca, Jennie Goossens as Calphurnia, Peter Finch as Mark Antony, Dennis Shaw as Soothsayer, Patrick Wymark as Brutus, Tenniel Evans as Cassius
   Living Shakespeare • 1962

ACT 1, SCENE 2, LINES 298–312
5. Narration by Derek Jacobi
6. Orson Welles as Cassius
   Mercury Theatre • 1938
7. John de Lancie as Cassius
   L.A. Theatre Works • 1995

ACT 2, SCENE 1, LINES 46–58
8. Narration by Derek Jacobi
9. George Coulouris as Brutus
   Mercury Theatre • 1938
10. John Bowe as Brutus
    Arkangel Shakespeare • 2003

ACT 2, SCENE 1, LINES 154–184
11. Narration by Derek Jacobi
12. Richard Baer as Decius, Orson Welles as Cassius, George Coulouris as Brutus
    Mercury Theatre • 1938
13. John Vickery as Decius, John de Lancie as Cassius, Stacey Keach as Brutus
    L.A. Theatre Works • 1995

Act 2, Scene 1, Lines 233–304

14. Narration by Derek Jacobi
15. Margaret Curtis as Portia, George Coulouris as Brutus
    Mercury Theatre • 1938
16. JoBeth Williams as Portia, Stacey Keach as Brutus
    L.A. Theatre Works • 1995

Act 2, Scene 2, Lines 13–56

17. Narration by Derek Jacobi
18. Shirley Dixon as Calphurnia, Michael Feast as Caesar
    Arkangel Shakespeare • 2003
19. Jennie Goossens as Calphurnia, John Moffatt as Caesar,
    Peter Williams as the Servant
    Living Shakespeare • 1962

Act 3, Scene 1, Lines 66–84

20. Narration by Derek Jacobi
21. Harold Gould as Caesar, Rudy Hornish as Cinna, John Vickery
    as Decius, Jack Coleman as Casca, Stacey Keach as Brutus
    L.A. Theatre Works • 1995
22. John Moffatt as Caesar, Peter Ellis as Cinna, Peter Williams
    as Decius, Brian Haines as Casca, Patrick Wymark as Brutus
    Living Shakespeare • 1962

Act 3, Scene 1, Lines 254–275

23. Narration by Derek Jacobi
24. Orson Welles as Mark Antony
    Mercury Theatre • 1938
25. Adrian Lester as Mark Antony
    Arkangel Shakespeare • 2003
26. Herbert Beerbohm Tree as Mark Antony
    Rare archival footage • 1906

ACT 3, SCENE 2, LINES 12–41

27. Narration by Derek Jacobi
28. George Coulouris as Brutus
    Mercury Theatre • 1938
29. Patrick Wymark as Brutus
    Living Shakespeare • 1962

ACT 3, SCENE 2, LINES 66–101

30. Narration by Derek Jacobi
31. Orson Welles as Mark Antony
    Mercury Theatre • 1938
32. Adrian Lester as Mark Antony
    Arkangel Shakespeare • 2003
33. Simon Russell Beale as Mark Antony
    Naxos • 1994

ACT 3, SCENE 3, LINES 1–34

34. Narration by Derek Jacobi
35. Richard Baer as Cinna the Poet
    Mercury Theatre • 1938
36. Arthur Hankey as Cinna the Poet and Lee Arenberg, Josh Fradon,
    and Marnie Mosiman as Plebeians
    L.A. Theatre Works • 1995

ACT 4, SCENE 2, LINES 137-170

37. Narration by Derek Jacobi
38. Orson Welles as Cassius, George Coulouris as Brutus
    Mercury Theatre • 1938
39. John de Lancie as Cassius, Stacey Keach as Brutus
    L.A. Theatre Works • 1995

ACT 5, SCENE 3, LINES 23–50

40. Narration by Derek Jacobi
41. Orson Welles as Cassius, Erskine Sanford as Pindarus
    Mercury Theatre • 1938
42. John de Lancie as Cassius, Paul Winfield as Pindarus
    L.A. Theatre Works • 1995

ACT 5, SCENE 5, LINES 31–51 AND LINES 67–74

43. Narration by Derek Jacobi
44. John Bowe and Adrian Lester
    Arkangel Shakespeare • 2003
45. Patrick Wymark and Peter Finch
    Living Shakespeare • 1962

46. Introduction to Speaking Shakespeare by Derek Jacobi
47. Speaking Shakespeare by Andrew Wade with Drew Cortese

48. Conclusion of the Sourcebooks Shakespeare *Julius Caesar*
    by Derek Jacobi

Featured Audio Productions

ORSON WELLES'S JULIUS CAESAR: The Mercury Theatre Production (1938–1939)

Julius Caesar	Edgar Barrier
Octavius Caesar	Edgar Barrier
Marcus Antonius	Orson Welles
M. Aemil Lepidus	Walter Ash
Publius	Jack Berry
Popilius Lena	Jack Berry
Marcus Brutus	George Coulouris
Caius Cassius	Orson Welles
Casca	Everett Sloane
Cinna the Conpirator	Guy Kingsley
Trebonius	J. Arthur Kennedy
Ligarius	Erskine Sanford
Decius Brutus	Richard Baer
Metellus Cimber	Seymour Milbert
Flavius	J. Arthur Kennedy
Marullus	William Alland
Calphurnia	Anna Stafford
Portia	Margaret Curtis
Lucilius	Stephen Roberts
Titinius	J. Arthur Kennedy
Messala	Stephen Roberts
Young Cato	William Alland
Volumnius	Jack Berry
Clitus	J. Arthur Kennedy
Lucius	Gay Kingsley
Pindarus	Erskine Sanford
Artemidorus	Everett Sloane
Cinna the Poet	Richard Baer
Narrator	Orson Welles

Living Shakespeare (1962)

Julius Caesar	John Moffatt
Casca	Brian Haines
Calphurnia	Jennie Goossens
Marcus Antonius	Peter Finch
Soothsayer	Denis Shaw
Marcus Brutus	Patrick Wymark
Cassius	Tenniel Evans
Narrator	Dennis Vance
Lucius	Bill Horsley
Decius Brutus	Peter Williams
Cinna	Peter Ellis
Trebonius	George Yeatman
Servant	Peter Williams
Publius	Denis Shaw
Metellus Cimber	Brian Hawksley
3rd Citizen	Dennis Shaw
2nd Citizen	Dennis Shaw
1st Citizen	Brian Haines
4th Citizen	Bill Horsley
Massala	Brian Hawksley
Octavius Caesar	George Yeatman
Pindarus	Brian Haines
Titinius	Peter Ellis

L.A. Theatre Works Presents Julius Caesar (1995)

Marcus Brutus	Stacey Keach
Cassius	John de Lancie
Marc Anthony	Richard Dreyfuss
Caesar	Harold Gould
Casca	Jack Coleman
Portia	JoBeth Williams
Calphurnia	Bonnie Bedelia
Murellus	Kelsey Grammer
Flavius, Artemidorus	John Randolph
Octavius	Arye Gross
Popilius, Pindarus, Antony's Servant	Paul Winfield
Decius Brutus, Lucilius	John Vickery
Soothsayer, Ligarius	Basil Langton
Metellus Cimber	David Birney
Cicero, Messala	George Murdock
Cobbler, Titinius	James Morrison
Lucius, Strato	Andy White
Cinna, Messenger, Poet, Soldier	Rudy Hornish
Plebeian, Claudio, soldier	Lee Arenberg
Volumnius, Caesar's Servant, Octavius's Servant	Jon Matthews
Carpenter, Young Cato, Plebeian, Soldier	Josh Fradon
Trebonius, Varrus, Soldier, Clitus	Paul Mercier
Publius, Cinna the poet, Dardanius, Lepidus	Arthur Hankey
Plebeian	Marnie Mosiman

The Complete Arkangel Shakespeare (2003)

Julius Caesar	Michael Feast
Brutus	John Bowe
Mark Antony	Adrian Lester
Cassius	Geoffrey Whitehead
Portia	Estelle Kohler
Octavius	Jonathan Tayler
Calphurnia	Shirley Dixon
Casca	Keith Drinkel
Flavius	Bill Homewood
Marullus	Will Keen
Pindarus	Sean Baker
Lucilius	Nicholas Murchie
Artemidorus	Paul Goodwin
Cinna the Poet	John Dallimore
Soothsayer	David King

Great Speeches and Soliloquies (1994)
Performed by Simon Russell Beale

Note from the Series Editors

For many of us, our first and only encounter with Shakespeare was in school. We may recall that experience as a struggle, working through dense texts filled with unfamiliar words. However, those of us who were fortunate enough to have seen a play performed have altogether different memories. It may be of an interesting scene or an unusual character, but it is most likely a speech. Often, just hearing part of one instantly transports us to that time and place. "Friends, Romans, countrymen, lend me your ears," "But, soft! What light through yonder window breaks?," "To sleep, perchance to dream," "Tomorrow, and tomorrow, and tomorrow."

The Sourcebooks Shakespeare series is our attempt to use the power of performance to help you experience the play. In it, you will see photographs from various productions, on film and on stage, historical and contemporary, known worldwide or in your community. You may recognize some actors that you didn't know were Shakespearean performers. You will see set drawings, costume designs, and scene edits, all reproduced from original notes. Finally, on the enclosed audio CD, you will hear scenes from the play as performed by some of the most accomplished Shakespeareans of our times. Often, we include multiple interpretations of the same scene, showing you the remarkable richness of the text. Hear the great Orson Welles in a 1938 recording reciting Mark Antony's famous speech. Compare that to Adrian Lester's recording, made in 2003. Listen to a modern American version with Richard Dreyfuss as Mark Antony. The actors create different worlds, different characters, different meanings.

As you read the text of the play, you can consult explanatory notes for definitions of unfamiliar words and phrases or words whose meanings have changed. These notes appear on the left pages, next to the text of the play. The audio, photographs, and other production artifacts augment the notes and they too are indexed to the appropriate lines. Use the pictures to see how others have staged a particular scene and get ideas on costumes, scenery, blocking, and other aspects of performance. As for the audio, each track represents a particular interpretation of a scene. Sometimes, a passage that's difficult to comprehend opens up when you hear it out loud. Furthermore, when you hear more than one version, you gain a keener understanding of the characters. Was Brutus acting for the good of Rome? Was Caesar a tyrant? The actors made their choices and so can you. You may even come up with your own interpretation.

The text of the play, the definitions, the production notes, the audio—all of these work together, and they are also there for your enjoyment. Because the audio is excerpts of performances, it is meant to entertain. When you see a passage with an associated clip, you can read along as you hear the actors perform the scenes for you. Or, you can sit back, close your eyes, and listen, and then go back and reread the text with a new perspective. Finally, since the text is actually a script, you may find yourself reciting the lines out loud and doing your own performance!

You will undoubtedly notice that some of the audio does not exactly match the text. Also, there are photographs and facsimiles of scenes that aren't in your edition. There are many reasons for this, but foremost among them is the fact that Shakespeare scholarship continues to move forward and the prescribed ways of dealing with and interpreting text is always changing. Thus a play that was edited and published in the 1930s will be different from one published in 2005. It may also surprise you to know that there frequently isn't one definitive early edition of each play. *Julius Caesar* was first printed in 1623 as part of the First Folio; it appeared in three more Folio editions after that. Currently, most scholars base their texts on the First Folio edition, and we have followed suit. Finally, artists have their own interpretation of the play and they too cut and change lines and scenes according to their vision. Orson Welles, in his Mercury Theatre production, famously added lines from *Coriolanus* and *Henry VIII* to his version.

The ways in which *Julius Caesar* has been presented have varied considerably through the years. We've included essays in the book to give you glimpses into the range of the productions, showing you how other artists have approached the play and providing examples of just what changes were made and how. Artistic Director Jeffrey Horowitz writes about the Theatre for a New

Audience's 2003 production, set in a stark, contemporary world where the drama of politics and power is played out against shifting planes of concrete. "In Production," an essay by our text editor, Robert Ormsby, provides an overview of how the play has been performed through the years: from its early history, where the portrayal of Brutus as the philosophical, restrained hero of the play was established; Orson Welles's innovative, blatantly political Mercury Theatre production in 1938 (subtitled *Death of a Dictator*); Mankiewicz's 1953 film starring Marlon Brando; and back to the stage with Peter Hall and the RSC in 1995. In "O, What a Fall Was There, My Countrymen!" Douglas Lanier discusses how the reputation of this play in popular culture has risen and fallen through the years. Though its status in Western pop culture has slipped, he cites adaptations of the play to world theatrical styles, including African, Kathakali (Indian), and Kabuki (Japanese) theater. Finally, for the actor in you, (and for those who want to peek behind the curtain), we have two essays that you may find especially intriguing. Andrew Wade, voice coach of the Royal Shakespeare Company for sixteen years, shares his point of view on how to understand the text and speak it. You can also listen in on him working with an actor on one of Brutus's speeches; perhaps you too can learn the art of speaking Shakespeare. The last essay is from an interview we conducted in which we talked to each member of a cast, asking the actors about their characters and relationships. We found it fascinating to hear what they had to say on various topics, for example: was Brutus a patriot or a murderer? Was Caesar a hero, or a tyrant who deserved death? The characters come to life in a way that's different from reading the book or watching a performance.

One last note, we are frequently asked why we didn't include the whole play, either in audio or video. While we enjoy the plays and are avid theatergoers, we are trying to do something more with the audio (and the production notes and the essays) than just presenting them to you. In fact, our goal is to provide you tools that will enable you to explore the play on your own, from many different directions. Our hope is that the different pieces of audio, the voices of the actors, and the classic production photos and notes will all engage you and illuminate the play on many levels, so that you can construct your own understanding and create your own "production," a fresh interpretation unique to you.

Though the productions we reference and the audio clips we have included are but a miniscule sample of the play's history, we hope they encourage you to further delve into the works of Shakespeare. New editions of the play come out yearly; movie adaptations are regularly being produced; there are hundreds of theater groups in the U.S. alone; and performances could be going on right in your backyard. We echo the words of noted writer and poet Robert Graves, who said, "The remarkable thing about Shakespeare is that he is really very good–in spite of all the people who say he is very good."

We welcome you now to The Sourcebooks Shakespeare edition of *Julius Caesar.*

Dominique Raccah and Marie Macaisa
Series Editors

Introduction to the Sourcebooks Shakespeare *Julius Caesar*
Derek Jacobi

track 1

In Production:

Julius Caesar THROUGH THE YEARS

Robert Ormsby

With only brief interruptions, *Julius Caesar* has been part of the Western the-atrical repertoire ever since Charles II reopened the theaters at the time of his Restoration in 1660. Proof of *Caesar*'s popularity in England (before the Civil War closed the theaters in 1642) exists in several documents. The Swiss tourist Thomas Platter witnessed what seemed to be Shakespeare's play on September 21, 1599, and we can be relatively certain about three other per-formances: circa 1612–13 (as part of the celebrations for James I's daughter's wedding), 1636–37, and 1638. We know of the familiarity with *Caesar* in the Elizabethan and Stuart-era theater world from references in the drama of Shakespeare's contemporaries, as well as in two dedicatory poems (in 1623 and 1640) by a fellow member of the King's Men theatrical company, Leonard Digges.

Caesar would have fired the imagination of Shakespeare's audiences. In the Renaissance, it was through adaptations of the classical past that early modern Europeans came to terms with contemporary political, social, and artistic concerns. Although the play takes place in Rome of 44 AD, Shakespeare adapts the struggle between tyranny and republicanism to Elizabethan frames of reference. Not only do his Romans speak English blank verse, they make references to doublets and paginated books (which were unavailable to ancient Romans) and frequently assume a Christian world view, evident in such English-specific puns as the Cobbler's reference to restoring "soles." (1.1.14)

Just as importantly, *Caesar* fully exploits the potential of Shakespeare's theater. The bare Elizabethan stage was well-suited to the play's fluid changes of locale and allowed the actors' poetic speeches to set the tone of each scene. *Caesar* no doubt fed the audience's appetite for gripping dialogue with its astonishing variety of verbal exchanges: the Soothsayer's public warning of Caesar about the Ides of March; intimate yet intense domestic scenes between Brutus and Portia and Caesar and Calphurnia; the conspirators' eloquently heated debate (particularly Brutus's and Cassius's confrontation in 4.2); the compelling rhetoric of Brutus's and Antony's funeral speeches (3.2); and the boasting taunts that the opposing Roman generals hurl at each other in 5.1.

Furthermore, evidence suggests other kinds of dramatic opportunities for Shakespeare's actors and audiences. In his dedicatory verses to a 1640 edition of Shakespeare's poems, Digges writes of the confrontation between Brutus and Cassius before the battle at Phillipi, in which the two men half-draw their swords in anger. Specifically, he recalls the episode's effect on the spectators: "oh how the Audience, / Were ravish'd, with what wonder they went thence. . . ." Platter, meanwhile, praised the actors for dancing "according to their custom with extreme elegance." He was referring to the Elizabethans' conventional post-performance jig, a practice that, to our modern theatrical expectations, seems entirely out of place at the conclusion of a tragedy.

Clues within the script point to theatrical effects. The thunder of 2.1, Lucius's music in 4.2, and the trumpets throughout all help build and diminish the levels of dramatic tension. The appearance of Caesar's ghost is the culminating embodiment of the terrifying supernatural visions Casca and Calphurnia report with such vivid imagery. Similarly, the lurid spectacles of the play's murders and suicides would have had considerable effect in a theater that favored visual excitement over scenic realism.

EARLY STAGE PRODUCTIONS, FROM THE SEVENTEENTH TO THE NINETEENTH CENTURY

When regular theatrical performances began again in 1660, England was a very different nation from the one that witnessed *Caesar*'s 1599 Globe performance. Not only had its lengthy conflict, driven by the same imperatives that motivate the characters in Shakespeare's tragedy, led to the execution of Charles I, its theater had changed, too. Officially sanctioned performances of spoken drama took place exclusively indoors; these productions were lit by candle; London was dominated by two companies; and women began acting professionally. From the little we know of *Caesar*'s history from 1660 to the mid-1680s, the play seems to have been performed fairly regularly, likely in something close to the 1623 Folio state of the script. The great English actor Thomas Betterton (1635–1710) secured the tragedy's place in the repertoire, acting Brutus from 1694–1707, originally against William Smith's powerful Cassius. Together, they established the enduring convention of portraying Brutus as the philosophical, restrained hero of the play in contrast to the high-tempered Cassius.

While the play fell into disfavor for several decades after 1751, leading actors Barton Booth (1681–1733) and James Quin (1693–1766) kept the Betterton tradition alive, helping make *Caesar* very popular in the first half of the eighteenth century, with over 163 performances between 1700 and 1751. Not much is clear about the acting texts used, but the play was not so altered from its Folio state as other Shakespeare plays were in the era. Generally, changes to the play helped solidify several traditions: language deemed unbecoming a tragedy was reduced; Cinna the Poet and the Poet at Brutus's tent in 4.2 disappeared; and the crowds dwindled to just a few characters. Eighteenth-century staging conditions, meanwhile, encouraged swift performances, and the simplicity of scenery and the apron stage that jutted out into the audience encouraged both a focus on the actor and a close relationship between the performers and the audience.

The actor-manager John Philip Kemble (1757–1823), one of the most important figures in English theater history, restored *Caesar* to the repertoire while increasing Brutus's centrality in the tragedy with a monumental performance of the role. Kemble's 1812 Covent Garden production, revived regularly until his retirement in 1817, set the scenographic and textual patterns for English and American *Caesar* stagings throughout the century.

Kemble built on the eighteenth-century theatre's candlelit stage (with flats of painted scenery that slid on grooves to change locales) and developed the staging of *Caesar* enormously. He posed his greatly increased number of supernumeraries (minor actors in crowd scenes) like scenery against beautifully painted flats that depicted the opulence of Imperial Rome. Kemble also utilized the downstage apron for the stunning spectacle of processions and discoveries, providing more intimate effects. His Shakespearean productions grew from his belief that art should improve upon nature, not simply copy it. The result was a "toga and sandals" *Caesar* with magnificent scenery of an idealized Rome.

In Kemble's productions, the speaking was studied and declamatory, while the action was stately, with little hectic movement. For instance, the assassination was a carefully orchestrated affair, while the battle scenes were carefully depicted with small processions and the flourish of trumpets. Yet despite Kemble's avowed veneration of Shakespeare's text, he imposed a unity on the play he thought missing in the original, cutting the script more than it ever had been by removing 450 lines and fourteen speaking roles. He reduced the contradictions in Antony's character and gave him more followers to create a balance between his faction and the conspirators'. Kemble also considerably played down Brutus's weaknesses in order to make him the idealized philosophical, stoic patriot. This is clearly demonstrated in his non-Shakespearean death speech (replacing 5.5.50–51), where he declares his sense of the justness of his cause and his love of country. Though Kemble was ably assisted his brother Charles (1775–1854) in the role of Antony and Charles Mayne Young (1777–1856) as Cassius, the show belonged to the

Edwin Booth
Mary Evans Picture Library

actor-manager, who played Brutus as he saw him: epically stoic and digni-fied. Reviewers admired his heroic physique and his characteristic ability to project nobility with a clear speaking voice and majestic poses. Kemble undoubtedly influenced most major nineteenth-century *Caesar* productions: versions of his text were widely acted; his themes, such as individual spiri-tual struggle trumping partisan political interests, held sway; and (with some exceptions) Brutus remained the play's focal point.

One such production, the foremost nineteenth-century American inter-pretation, was that of actor-manager Edwin Booth (1833–93), which opened at Booth's Theater on December 25, 1871. *Caesar*'s political dilemma seemed perfectly suited to Booth's American audiences, who could have drawn an analogy between the conspirators' actions and their own republican aspira-tions, as well as find in Caesar a model of British tyranny. The play might have also had a personal resonance for Booth: he first played Brutus in 1864 alongside the Antony of his brother, John Wilkes Booth, shortly before the latter assassinated President Abraham Lincoln.

Artistically and morally conservative, Edwin Booth sought to ennoble his audiences with plays from a classical repertoire, most importantly Shakespeare. Like Kemble, he claimed to value Shakespeare's text, yet his script was actually an altered version of Kemble's. Booth divided the action into six acts, each a discrete episode that he opened with a striking image and closed with a dramatic curtain drop. Generally, his cuts tighten and speed the action, with many alterations affecting Brutus (most notably, he gave himself an additional pair of showy entrances, in 1.2 and 5.2).

Booth employed the talented scenic artist Charles Witham to create beau-tiful vistas of Rome (again Imperial rather than Republican) for stunning opening curtains, such as the magnificent images of a square in 1.1 and the Forum in 3.2. Booth also used as many as two hundred supernumeraries for the production's sumptuous processions. Furthermore, his technologically advanced theater permitted scenic effects unavailable to the early nine-teenth-century stage, including the startlingly luminescent appearance of Caesar's ghost in 4.2. The production's highlight was the assassination scene. An embellishment of Jean Louis Gérôme's well-known 1867 painting *La Mort de César*, Booth's tableau of the murder was a remarkable study in visual composition and the arrangement of performers as scenery.

Jean Louis Gérôme's well-known 1867 painting *La Mort de César*
Mary Evans Picture Library

Reviewers did not find the effect of Booth's five-foot-seven frame in period costuming ideally suited to the heroic bearing they demanded of Brutus. Still, the actor used his expressive eyes and the wide emotional range of his rich voice to lend his Brutus more realistic feeling than Kemble had mustered. Though his was an uncomplicated hero of stern, authoritative dignity, Booth also portrayed a tortured soul, torn between personal friendship and patriotism. During the record-breaking eighty-five-night run, Booth demonstrated his versatility by switching roles and was the first actor to play Brutus, Antony, and Cassius in a single production.

ORSON WELLES AND THE MERCURY THEATER (1937)
By the time Orson Welles mounted the Mercury Theater's modern dress production in 1937, the world from which epic-heroic *Caesars* emerged had been swept aside by the tumult of World War One, the Russian Revolution, and the Great Depression. The theater had witnessed the rise of Naturalism, the avant-garde, and experiments in Elizabethan performance techniques, while advancements in lighting and sound technology helped create competition from film and radio.

Welles formed the Mercury Theater with John Houseman after leaving the Federal Theater Project. The Mercury gathered a left-leaning audience and was largely supported by New York's liberal and communist organizations and press. This constituency was fervently anti-Fascist, and Welles used his blatantly political *Caesar*, subtitled *Death of a Dictator*, to show the dangers of dictatorship and the mob's violent complicity in the totalitarian state. This *Caesar* cut huge portions of Shakespeare's text: Cicero, Octavius, Lepidus, Caesar's Ghost, and the Portia-Lucius-Soothsayer scene (2.4) are gone; the conspirators no longer wash their hands in Caesar's blood (3.1); and the final act is reduced to a mere thirty-two lines. Yet this swift-moving text also reveals several innovations: Welles added lines from Shakespeare's *Coriolanus* and *Henry VIII*; the play opens ominously with the Soothsayer's Ides of March warning; the Roman Citizens' involvement in the Forum scene is increased; and the Cinna the Poet scene is finally restored.

In the tradition of actor-manager-driven *Caesars*, Welles directed and took the role of Brutus, playing him as a reserved, honest, and noble man, seen by critics as a waffling liberal university professor forced finally to act against tyranny. The performance was strongly supported by Martin Gabel's Cassius, George Coulouris's Antony, and the Caesar of Joseph Holland (who bore a convenient resemblance to Italian dictator Benito Mussolini). The crowd was also vital to the production: they played large roles in the Forum and Cinna the Poet episodes, and buttressed Marc Blitzstein's score (played on a tremendously loud Hammond organ) with offstage shouts and the sounds of marching jack-boots.

Yet the production's design was its most revolutionary feature. In the theater's bare three-level stage backed by a blood-red brick wall, designer Jean Rosenthal's evocative play of light and shadow, with its cinematic fades and focus on specific actors, defined the production's scenography. Welles used the light to effect rapid scene changes, to draw comparisons between Antony's Forum speech and Hitler's rallies at Nuremberg (with the crowd standing in semi-darkness, far below the ten-foot-tall rostrum), and to create the show's terrifying murder of Cinna the Poet, in which Norman Lloyd's Cinna walks into a circle of light, and is slowly surrounded by the bloodthirsty crowd who step out of the darkness as if from nowhere.

AT THE MOVIES: JOSEPH MANKIEWICZ'S *Julius Caesar* (1953)

John Houseman provides a bridge between the Mercury Theater *Caesar* and Joseph Mankiewicz's Oscar-nominated 1953 film of the play. Houseman produced both versions and tried to link them by arguing that Mankiewicz's use of black-and-white film was intended to evoke Fascist newsreels. However, where Welles made overt political allusions to Hitler and Mussolini, Mankiewicz's film returns to period costuming and only subtly advances any political agenda its producers might have had. Furthermore, with the Cold War raging in Europe and Southeast Asia, audiences were more likely to draw analogies between Shakespeare's characters and figures like Joseph

George Coulouris as Mark Antony in Orson Welles's 1937 Mercury Theater production
Billy Rose Theatre Collection, The New York Public Library for the Performing Arts, Astor, Lenox and Tilden Foundations

Stalin, General Douglas MacArthur, and Senator Joseph McCarthy, chair of the House Un-American Activities Committee (HUAC), whose chilling influence was felt throughout Hollywood.

Nevertheless, the film does carry an anti-demagogic message. In addition to numerous statues of Caesar, the film abounds in the sorts of Roman imagery (particularly eagles) that had been appropriated as Fascist emblems in the 1930s and '40s and would have been read as such in 1953. Mankiewicz also uses the steep inclines and platforms in the Forum scene to suggest Rome's power structure, a structure he emphasizes during Antony's (played by Marlon Brando) oration by shooting downwards at the crowd over his shoulder, or upwards at Antony from the crowd's perspective. The camera captures Brando's calculating look when he pauses in his speech, and we see the smile of satisfaction on his face when he turns from the rioting citizens to ascend the stairs away from them. Finally, Mankiewicz used the authoritarian theme in Miklos Rozsa's musical score for both Caesar's and Antony's scenes, stressing the continuity between the two leaders.

Despite the fact that its large realistic crowds (of up to 1,200 extras) and its fifth-act full-scale battle scene place this *Caesar* firmly within the classical/Biblical Hollywood epic genre, the film is very much an actor's picture. Mankiewicz frequently filmed actors from the eye level in medium- and long-shots to fill the frame with a human point of view, and there were relatively few editing techniques that overtly drew attention to the medium itself. The movie's star power also kept the focus on the actors. Marlon Brando, whose popularity soared with his portrayal of Stanley Kowalski in the film of *A Streetcar Named Desire* (1951), drew undeserved criticism for his accomplished verse speaking of Antony's lines. The conspirators, once read by Americans as synonymous with anti-British sentiment, were lead by English actors James Mason, as Brutus, and John Gielgud, who reprised his Stratford-upon-Avon performance of Cassius. Mason's upper-class tones and Gielgud's musical delivery of lines accentuated their foreignness in a film dominated by American speech. This foreignness perhaps reflected (if unintentionally) the political marginalization that many in Hollywood felt at a time when colleagues and friends lived under constant threat of the HUAC Blacklist.

BACK ON STAGE: PETER HALL AND THE ROYAL SHAKESPEARE COMPANY (1995)

Much postwar Shakespearean theater owes more obvious debts to the trappings of Welles's production than it does to Mankiewicz's film—indeed "fascist" *Caesars* are now cliché. More importantly, this era of Shakespearean production has been characterized by a search for "contemporary relevance." Nowhere has this search for relevance been more fervently invoked than at the Royal Shakespeare Company (RSC), created in 1960 from Stratford-upon-Avon's Shakespeare Memorial Theater. During his eight-year reign, founding artistic director Peter Hall built the RSC into one of the world's foremost repertoire companies, with a reputation for claiming to match authoritative readings of Shakespeare's texts with productions that speak urgently to the modern world.

Hall's 1995 *Caesar* was, in fact, closer to the 1953 film in its politics and design. Besides the program's implied connection between the play and the Balkan war of the 1990s, Hall emphasized, in preview newspaper stories, the relationship between *Caesar* and the Tory party's leadership vote, which took place the day before opening night: "All those people lying through their teeth saying, 'We are doing it for the good of the country' and 'my duty' and 'the air must be cleared.' What's interesting to me is that the problems of leadership, ambition, freedom, and loyalty were just the same for Shakespeare looking at ancient Rome as they are for us watching *Newsnight*."

The production's design, however, kept Hall's political message vague, and left audiences to discover relevance to contemporary political situations for themselves. John Gunter's historically non-specific set architecture of moveable black panels and white steps was given a Roman feel from Deirdre Clancy's period costuming (red togas for senators, white for Caesar and Antony, and gray clothes for the people) and from Gunter's own use of Roman motifs, such as a golden lion atop one of the panels and an oversized eagle and bird's claw that decorated the platform. Following earlier productions (such as Jiri Frejka's 1936 Prague *Caesar* and Trevor Nunn's mounting of the play at Stratford-upon-Avon in 1972), a large image of Caesar hung over the action to suggest his domination and the threat of his tyrannical ambitions. Gunter and Hall spilled stage blood liberally throughout the production: Christopher Benjamin's Caesar bled profusely when stabbed; a pail of red liquid was thrown down the stairs after Cinna the Poet was lynched; and Caesar's image bleeds as it looms above the action in the final scenes.

The director was perhaps more concerned with the actors' delivery of Shakespeare's text, which he staged without an intermission and apparently did not cut, than he was with the show's design. Half-jokingly labeled an "iambic fundamentalist" by his colleagues, Hall has strict beliefs about the meaning encoded in Shakespeare's meter, and Julian Glover, who played Cassius, tells how Hall would "conduct" speech rehearsals with his text on a music stand and a pencil for a baton. Yet, while reviewers noted the pace of the delivery and action, they complained about the actors' failure to link speech with convincing and nuanced characterization, especially John Nettles's Brutus and Hugh Quarshie's Antony. Critics were also dismayed by the performances of several dozen unpaid supernumeraries, a variation of Hall's attempt to bring audience members into the action in his 1984–85 National Theater *Coriolanus.*

The RSC *Caesar* demonstrates that orthodoxy about decoding meaning supposedly embedded in Shakespeare's texts, no matter how well-intentioned, does not always result in compelling theater. Though Kemble and Welles altered Shakespeare's text and were far removed from Shakespeare's staging techniques and historical moment, they understood what "worked" for their times and in their theaters. No matter how we admire Shakespeare the writer for what we encounter on the page and in performance, his fortunes rise and fall according to what readers, actors, directors, and audiences do in collaboration with the plays. Of course, many still feel the urge to work with Shakespeare, and *Caesar* shows no sign of losing favor with audiences: since 1995, there have been more than one hundred noteworthy productions of the play. For now, it seems that *Caesar,* with its compelling political debate, its poignant struggles of personal conscience, and its richly dense poetry, will continue to find eager theatrical collaborators.

As Performed

Jeffrey Horowitz

On January 19, 2003, Theatre for a New Audience (TFANA) opened its production of Shakespeare's *Julius Caesar*, directed by Karin Coonrod, in New York City at the 299-seat Lucille Lortel Theatre. As the artistic director of TFANA, I had invited Karin to direct *Julius Caesar*. Let me tell you how we worked with Karin and a company of artists to realize this play.

First, a brief word about Theatre for a New Audience. Founded in 1979, TFANA is a leading classical theater rooted in Shakespeare. "New Audience" in our name means an audience open to discovery. We want our productions to open minds and get audiences to listen to and think about our world. We want audiences to find in our productions the present in the past and the past in the present. The great director Peter Brook says: "Shakespeare doesn't belong to the past. If his material is valid, it is valid now." This doesn't necessarily mean playing in modern dress (although our production of *Julius Caesar* was, in fact, in modern dress). It means uncovering the connections between Shakespeare and our world.

Karin and I first worked together in January 2000 when she directed our production of Shakespeare's history play *King John*. Karin's *King John* was spare, no frills, and fast-moving, and most of the actors played several parts. *Julius Caesar* employed a similar directorial approach. It too was unadorned, fast, and almost all the actors played multiple roles, many as part of an ensemble called the citizens. In our production, more than half the cast, the director, the designers, and the vocal coaches shared artistic values and had previously worked with the theater. Karin's *Julius Caesar* featured an ensemble instead of individual star actors and was rooted in the political climate of New York City and America in 2003.

THE PRODUCTION

For us, *Julius Caesar* resonated with two momentous events in American history: George W. Bush's contested presidential election in 2000 and the terrorist attacks of September 11, 2001. It was part of Theatre for a New Audience's 2003 season, in which each of the three plays we produced shared the common theme of betrayal: Moliere's *Don Juan;* Shakespeare's *Julius Caesar;* and *The General from America,* a contemporary play by Richard Nelson about Benedict Arnold, an officer in the American Revolutionary War whose name has become synonymous with "traitor." In contemplating the betrayal of America, Arnold asks, "What is a traitor? What is an American? Can one betray a country that is betraying itself?" In *Julius Caesar,* a similar question is posed: who betrayed Rome, Caesar or the conspirators?

In the summer of 2002, ten months after the attacks, Karin and I began working on *Julius Caesar.* Karin spoke about Ground Zero: the blasted concrete, twisted iron, American flags, police, passionate crowds, and bright floodlights. She noted that Ground Zero was always lit by harsh lights as the rubble was removed day and night.

Other American events informed our conversations. Civil liberties were limited in the name of national security: American citizens had been jailed as "enemy combatants" and a writ of habeas corpus denied; some journalists and politicians were accused of being unpatriotic when they questioned the president's policies. We often heard the word "patriotism," but it was not at all clear what that word meant. In a June 2002 edition of *U.S.News & World Report,* the lead story discussed the statistic "93 percent of Americans consider themselves to be patriotic" and considered the questions "Who is a patriot?" and "What does patriotism demand of us?"

Julius Caesar is, of course, a great, enduring play about politics and politicians, their values and their humanity. Although Caesar was assassinated March 15, 44 B.C., and Shakespeare explored the consequences of this act, the play is not about an actual society. The realities of the contested presidential election of 2000, the loss of civil liberties, and the horror of the terrorist attacks are more complex than any play can convey. But, in being aware of these events, Karin and I had a context for imagining the great debate the play raises: were the conspirators patriots and Caesar a tyrant, or was Caesar a hero and the conspirators murderers?

Logo

Long before rehearsals started, graphic artist Milton Glazer designed the logo that would communicate the essence of the production to potential ticket buyers. Karin described to Milton early images she had of the play. She talked about how the ancient and the modern came together in the gray stone of sculpture and how many cities all over the world in different times have busts of their Caesars—archetypal patriarchal leaders—carved from gray stone in public places. What gave life to the gray stone, for her, would be the red from Pompeian and Roman frescoes against a monochromatic gray palate. The red in the stone also reminded her of Ground Zero, where many American flags flew: red, white, and blue against a background of rubble. This inspired Milton's logo: a bust of a Caesar with blood seeping out of the stone. It also inspired the setting.

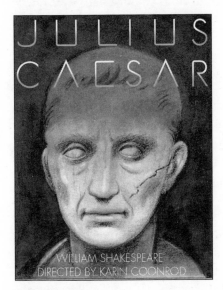

Logo by Milton Glazer

Setting

We thought about the famous Orson Welles production of 1937 that linked the play to the threat of fascism; Caesar was likened to Mussolini and the Roman tribunes wore brown shirts. In what year and what period should our own production of *Julius Caesar* be set? In what place? Should it be realistic and in a particular time? Or should it be in a world that is imagined and not literal? And, in either case, how did Shakespeare imagine Rome? What kind of city was it?

These vital questions inform every aspect of the production: how the play looks, how the actors behave, how the audience thinks about the production.

Karin wanted the production to be modern, but not historically explicit. The gray stone was essential, as it connected the ancient past and the present. The set designer, Douglas Stein, created a deceptively simple design. The floor was gray, concrete-like. Suspended from the ceiling, three massive slabs of "concrete" (it was plaster on wood, but looked like concrete), each eight feet high by one foot deep by thirty feet wide (the length of the stage) were hung in front of each other like curtains. There were several feet between each slab. The slabs could move up and down. If all three slabs were down, the depth of stage was very shallow and it felt claustrophobic. But, if the slabs were raised, the stage was deep.

These slabs were abstract. We could be anywhere. No scenery was needed for the many locales of the play; the action could move quickly. I was concerned, however, that we needed more variety. I asked, for example, why there wasn't an upstage balcony for the orations of Brutus and Mark Antony when they address the citizens. Karin replied that she wanted to flip the vantage point initially: Antony was to begin in the audience, speaking to the citizens who were on stage looking out at him. Thus, the audience would see the citizens' reactions. As the speech progressed, Antony would climb up on stage to be with the citizens, talking to them rather than orating. As he continued, he would go behind a concrete slab, climb a ladder leaning over the slab, and speak down to the citizens and out to the theatergoers. It was an unconventional staging that made the scene fresh.

Karin and the set designer felt that the concrete slabs and floor would work for all locations in the play: Rome, the homes of Caesar and Brutus, the Senate, the streets, and the war. There was to be no front curtain and, in the early scene when Caesar returns victorious from civil wars in Spain, the audience sees only concrete—no ornamentation, nothing soft. Caesar's authority and power was explicitly communicated. Rome was fortified, elegant, and modern, but it also felt like a prison.

LIGHTING

David Weiner's lighting supported this vision. Sometimes, the lights made the stage feel like a restless city at night; sometimes, when aimed at the audience, they created that feeling of being caught in the glare of floodlights. Even in intimate, domestic scenes, the light felt harsh, never calm or soft.

The concrete was a brilliant contrast to the one dramatic use of color. What the audience couldn't see was a trough in the floor. When Caesar was stabbed it filled with "blood." The conspirators bathed their hands in it and raised them, crying

> *Liberty! Freedom! Tyranny is dead!*
> *Liberty, freedom, and enfranchisement!*

Karin believed there could be no liberty with blood on one's hands. But, if Brutus is correct and Caesar is

> *as a serpent's egg*
> *Which, hatched, would, as his kind, grow mischievous,*

then are the conspirators right to kill him? The play offers no simple answer because it is about human beings, not abstractions.

Michael Rogers as Decius Brutus, Justin Campbell as Cinna, David Don Miller as Metellus Cimber, Thomas M. Hammond as Brutus, and Daniel Oreskes as Cassius
Photo by Gerry Goodstein

MUSIC

The composer Mark Bennett wrote original music and sound effects. Karin, Mark, and I all agreed that at the beginning of the play we wanted the audience to experience Caesar's power. When the lights rose, the entire company of eighteen actors moved in a line from upstage to downstage with Caesar at the center. Confetti tumbled from the ceiling. What made the scene eerie was the company singing an anthem to Caesar. Imagine a large American city celebrating returning troops from a war. No cheers. All you hear is everyone singing in unison our national anthem: "Oh, say can you see . . ."

Daniel Oreskes as Cassius, Hope Chernov as Calphurnia, Simeon Moore as Casca, Earl Hindman as Julius Caesar, Michael Rogers as Decius, Graham Winton as Mark Antony, and Thomas M. Hammond as Brutus
Photo by Gerry Goodstein

Mark found a speech in Latin by Cicero to Gaius Caesar that he set to rhythmic, original music. Of course, that song isn't in the text. In our production it was sung as a prologue. When Octavius triumphs at the end, the song repeated as a new cycle of power begins. The lyric began:

> *There is no genius so overflowing, no power of tongue or*
> *pen so lofty or so exuberant that it can adequately*
> *describe, let alone embellish your achievements.*

Shakespeare scholars have often noted the prominence of portents, ghosts, and the supernatural in *Julius Caesar*. There are also storms, thunder, cheering crowds, lions in the streets, chiming clocks, alarums, riots, and war. Mark created a turbulent, ominous score that gave the production the feel of a nightmare.

Costumes and Makeup

Catherine Zuber designed the costumes. Working from Karin's idea of gray stone, Catherine designed business suits in different shades of dark gray, dark ties, and white shirts for both the tribunes and the conspirators. Calphurnia and Portia wore elegant gray dresses. There were a few exceptions; for example, in his first entrance, Caesar wore a double-breasted dark overcoat with brass buttons, but no crown.

The effect was that the characters belonged to the same world. Today, of course, though many leaders wear suits, we don't usually think of these leaders as all being the same. We believe in individuality. We think we are different and free to do what we want. However, since all the characters in Karin's staging wore very similar clothing, the idea of individuality was undercut. This was also reinforced by the hair and makeup. All the men had similar haircuts. Black eyeliner outlined all the players' eyes, and the women also wore dark lipstick. The actors had to assert their individuality against the monochromatic palette. It was disquieting and made the audience question why the characters looked the same. Were there real differences between the conspirators and the tribunes? If the conspirators had prevailed, how different would Rome have been? Was the same story being told throughout history?

The Company

Eighteen actors formed the company. Other than those who played Caesar, Brutus, Cassius, and Mark Antony, all the actors played citizens as well as other characters. This was not merely doubling. It conveyed the fickle nature of the citizenry: the same actor who played Portia was also a citizen who rioted. Earl Hindman, a most genial mountain of a man who towered over everyone on stage, was Caesar. Thomas M. Hammond, a naturally thoughtful actor with great heart, played Brutus. Daniel Oreskes, an actor who effortlessly communicated unease, was Cassius. Graham Winton, gentle one moment and cruel the next, was Mark Antony. Michael Ray Escamilla played several roles, including a young Octavius.

Daniel Oreskes as Cassius and Thomas M. Hammond as Brutus
Photo by Gerry Goodstein

In rehearsals, the actors explored what it meant to fear tyranny and to lose liberty, what it meant to be patriotic, and what constituted Roman honor. We wrestled with the central questions of the play: did certain political conditions demand assassination? Who were the patriots?

Cicely Berry, director of voice at the Royal Shakespeare Company, along with Robert Neff Williams, an esteemed American vocal coach, worked with actors on Shakespeare's language. Cicely would often say that in Shakespeare, there is no period until the last word of the play. The characters are always trying to work out the problem. The approach made for spontaneous, vibrantly spoken text. Her approach fit in very well with Karin's cuts in the text. She divided the play into one act and twelve scenes and wanted it to play like an unstoppable juggernaut.

It's said that *Julius Caesar* is as much the tragedy of Brutus as Caesar. David Scott Kastan, professor in the humanities at Columbia University and general editor of *The Arden Shakespeare*, writes, "Both Brutus and Caesar try to impose their will upon history . . . Shakespeare's play works brilliantly as he shows us the tragedy of one impossible ideal sacrificed for another." Karin and the company interpreted the tragedy of *Julius Caesar* as the ongoing tragedy of violence and corruption in politics and what this does to the individual. They aimed to bring Shakespeare's tragedy to life in raw and direct ways. The stone bleeds and longs for something different.

"O, What a Fall Was There, My Countrymen!"

Julius Caesar IN POPULAR CULTURE

Douglas Lanier

Julius Caesar provides an interesting example of how reputations of individual Shakespeare plays rise and fall. For most of the nineteenth century and the first half of the twentieth, *Julius Caesar* ranked in the very top tier of Shakespeare's tragedies. An important reason for this—though certainly not the only one—is that the play was very widely taught in schools. Its speeches provided students with a model for public oratory. Antony's "Friends, Romans, countrymen" eulogy became one of the most admired and studied of all Shakespearean orations, a rhetorical set-piece often detached from the play itself, memorized by admirers and referenced frequently. However ambivalent, the play's message of resistance to tyranny, as well as its cautionary view of mob rule, resonated with the sorts of democratic ideals promulgated in American public schools and had affinities with concerns about the rise of popular culture in the early twentieth century. *Julius Caesar* also provided a quick introduction to a crucial moment in Roman history and thus a link to education in the classics that newly formed English departments—with Shakespeare at their symbolic center—were slowly displacing. And, perhaps not coincidentally, *Julius Caesar* offered an example of Shakespeare's artistic "seriousness," a play demonstrating the playwright's formidable classical learning and almost entirely unleavened by moments of his trademark humor. Because until the late 1960s *Julius Caesar* was a standard set-text in Anglo-American curricula (and to some extent in European curricula as well), during this period the play served as a widely shared touchstone.

PARODY AND POLITICS

Because it has been so often taught and performed, *Julius Caesar* has been regularly used for political commentary and is especially amenable to parody.

The assassination of Abraham Lincoln was widely compared to that of Caesar in contemporary newspaper accounts, particularly since John Wilkes Booth reportedly was so obsessed with Brutus. *Julius Snoozer*, an 1876 minstrel play performed by the San Francisco Minstrels, offered both political commentary and parody in the same package, using a blackface lampoon of Shakespeare's play to level criticism at New York City's corrupt Tammany Hall administration. The film *Up Pompeii* (1971), a British burlesque in the spirit of *A Funny Thing Happened on the Way to the Forum*, features an ongoing routine involving Ludicrus Sextus, a rich senator (played by Shakespearean actor Michael Hordern) who has been asked to address the Senate. Fittingly for this lampoon of a doddering, self-absorbed politician, Sextus's pompous oration begins "Friends, Pompeians, countrymen, lend me your feet," and he ends up delivering it as Pompeii is being destroyed.

Popular parodies often hinge on amateur or school *Caesar* performances that go disastrously wrong, itself an indication of how the play's tragic seriousness makes it especially vulnerable to burlesque, and, more importantly, an indication of how closely *Julius Caesar* is tied to Shakespeare experiences in school. "Beginner's Luck" (1935), one of the *Our Gang* serials, is typical of this kind of parody. Spanky, forced by his mother to give a rendition of Antony's funeral oration when she enters him in a local talent contest, is subjected to a peashooter barrage from his friends as he gives the speech, and he valiantly defends himself against his foes with a toy shield. Another indication that *Julius Caesar* is closely linked to school experiences with Shakespeare is the number of young adult magazines that feature versions of it. The very first adaptation of Shakespeare for *Classics Illustrated*, that venerable comic book series of high literary works, was *Julius Caesar* (#68, first published February 1950); its British counterpart, in the *Classics in Pictures* series, was published the next year. In its run, the *Classics Illustrated Julius Caesar* featured two quite different covers, the first a line drawing of Mark Antony delivering the funeral oration over Caesar's body, the second (appearing in 1960) a painting of two Roman soldiers in mid-swordfight. These covers suggest two ways in which this comic book version was marketed to young readers—as a crib for classroom assignments and as a boy's adventure story. *Julius Caesar* also holds the distinction of being the favorite Shakespearean target of lampoon for *Mad Magazine*, that stalwart of

American adolescent satire. The magazine's only parody of a Shakespeare film, of Joseph Mankiewicz's *Julius Caesar* (1953), was featured in its inaugural issue (1956), and parodies of Antony's funeral oration, in all manner of adolescent slang, have appeared periodically in its pages ever since.

Julius Caesar also served more serious purposes. Georges Méliès's 1907 short *Le Rêve de Shakespeare* (aka *Shakespeare Writing Julius Caesar*), shows Shakespeare overcoming a case of writer's block by falling asleep and dreaming the scene of Caesar's assassination, shown to us through Méliès's trademark trick photography. The film offers a mini-defense of silent movies, then a controversial medium, by aligning them with Shakespeare. Shakespeare's imagination, Méliès seems to argue, was fundamentally cinematic; the poet simply wrote down in words the pictures he first saw in his mind's eye. Méliès's choice of scene—the assassination of a tyrant—also makes the point that the movies (and Shakespeare) were fundamentally anti-elitist, an enemy of high culture, though of course Shakespeare's appearance on film lent the new medium an element of cultural prestige by association. Other silent film versions appeared in the next decade in England and America, bolstering the reputation of film as a "quality" medium. *Julius Caesar* was to serve the same purpose for radio and TV, with many prestigious productions of the play appearing in the early lives of both media.

The play also offered the potential for political criticism. In 1937, Orson Welles staged an anti-Nazi adaptation of *Julius Caesar* with his then-fledgling Mercury Theatre. When he revamped the production for radio the following year, he reframed it as a contemporary news broadcast, with excerpts from Shakespeare's source Plutarch delivered by newscaster H. V. Kaltenborn, whose voice was familiar to radio audiences from his reports of Hitler's assaults on Eastern Europe. In Britain after World War II, *Julius Caesar* was adapted as a thriller about lethal corporate aspirations in the film *An Honourable Murder* (1960). This film followed the lead of several earlier films of the 30s and 40s—*Little Caesar* (1931) prime among them—whose narratives of the rise and brutal fall of a gangster kingpin bore distant resemblances to elements in Shakespeare's play. And *Julius Caesar*, with its strong associations with stage productions, sometimes formed the backdrop for tales about actors, as in the silent melodrama *Stranded* (1913), in which a down-and-out aging Shakespearean saves a young girl from humiliation at the hands of an evil stage manager, or *The Phantom of 42nd Street* (1945), in which a detective exposes a murderer terrorizing a New York theater by including him in a rehearsal of the assassination scene from *Julius Caesar*.

Joseph Mankiewicz's 1953 film version of *Julius Caesar* merits special mention for several reasons. It was the first major attempt after the 1930s by an American film studio to mount a big-budget adaptation of a Shakespearean

The cast of Stuart Burge's 1970 production including Charlton Heston (Mark Antony),
Jason Robards (Brutus), John Gielgud (Julius Caesar), Richard Johnson (Cassius), Robert Vaughn (Casca),
Richard Chamberlain (Octavius Caesar), Diana Rigg (Portia), and Jill Bennett (Calpurnia)
Courtesy: Douglas Lanier

play, an attempt spurred on by the successes of Olivier's *Henry V* and *Hamlet*. The film brought together an impressive cast of acting luminaries from Britain and America. In fact, in retrospect it has a subtle Brit-versus-Yank quality in its pitting of John Gielgud (Cassius) and James Mason (Brutus) against Louis Calhern (Caesar) and Marlon Brando (Mark Antony). The film did much to establish the credentials of the young Brando (at the time only twenty-eight years old) as a serious actor, even though he brought bare-chested physicality and bad-boy associations to the role. The film was among the first of the "sword and sandal" film cycle, that series of classical and Biblical film epics which were to enjoy a vogue during the 50s and 60s. It also obliquely engaged contemporary politics. Its atmosphere of paranoia and retribution subtly suggest America under McCarthyism, where the fear of political conspiracies was answered by political demagoguery calculated to manipulate the masses.

The ease with which Brando's exceedingly cynical Antony turns the mob at Caesar's funeral, one of the actor's most electrifying performances, was so powerful that it became iconic for a generation, the subject of numerous popular homages and parodies. When Stuart Burge made his film version in 1970 with another all-star cast (with Charlton Heston and John Gielgud as Mark Antony and Julius Caesar respectively), the political subtext was considerably muted, the production values far more modest, and Heston's approach to Antony more conventionally heroic.

CAESAR, ANTONY, AND CLEOPATRA

On stage and screen the events of *Julius Caesar* have long been dovetailed with those of *Antony and Cleopatra*, with Caesar's tryst with Cleopatra serving as the opening act of a romantic epic, an act that ends with his assassination. A popular late nineteenth-century play, Victorien Sardou and Émile Moreau's *Cléopâtre* (1890), written for Sarah Bernhardt, formed the template for several adaptations to follow, particularly Cecil B. DeMille's *Cleopatra* (1934), Gabriel Pascal's *Caesar and Cleopatra* (1945, from George Bernard Shaw's play), and Joseph Mankiewicz's *Cleopatra* (1963). The last of these films, starring then-scandalous couple Elizabeth Taylor and Richard Burton, quickly became a notorious extravaganza that nearly bankrupted its film studio, Twentieth Century Fox, and spelled the end of the "sword and sandal" film cycle. Rex Harrison played Julius Caesar, and elements from Shakespeare's play–the constitution of the conspiracy, omens of Caesar's demise—appear in the film. Perhaps in deference to his *Julius Caesar* ten years earlier, Mankiewicz avoids directly rewriting Shakespeare's language in the play's most famous scenes. Cleopatra sees Caesar's assassination in a wordless vision, and Mark Antony's funeral oration is drowned out by the noise of the agitated mob. Mankiewicz's *Cleopatra* produced a brief cultural stir, prompting a surge in parodic allusions to Julius Caesar (and Cleopatra), among them *Carry On Cleo* (1964), an installment in the long-running British comedy series filmed on the same sets as Mankiewicz's production, and "Samantha's Caesar Salad" (1969), an episode of the American sitcom *Bewitched*.

In those adaptations that melded *Julius Caesar* with *Antony and Cleopatra*, Julius Caesar is conventionally portrayed as an older man who awakes Cleopatra's passions and political ambitions; by contrast, Mark Antony serves as her younger suitor over whom she wields erotic power. In most, all that survives of *Julius Caesar* are typically the warning about the Ides of March and the bloody nature of Caesar's assassination. This is, for example, the case with the recent television epic *Cleopatra* (1999), itself adapted from Margaret George's romance novel *The Memoirs of Cleopatra* (1997). (*The Spread of the Eagle*, a UK-produced TV mini-series from 1963, ambitiously sought to meld not just *Julius Caesar* and *Antony and Cleopatra*, but *Coriolanus* as well.) In reality, Julius Caesar was in his early fifties when he first encountered Cleopatra, Mark Antony was in his early forties (Shakespeare stresses Antony's age, not his youth). Indeed, the notion that Julius Caesar and Cleopatra were romantically involved remains disputed by historians of the period. It is clear that Shakespeare did not intend to link the two plays. He includes only a brief, equivocal allusion to Julius Caesar's relationship with Cleopatra in *Antony and Cleopatra* 2.6 and no reference at all to Cleopatra in *Julius Caesar*. Nevertheless, the association of these two legendary figures of the ancient world remains very strong in popular culture. The memorable circumstance of Caesar's death in Shakespeare's play has clearly influenced how that episode has been handled (and why it has been so often included) in popular chronicles of Cleopatra's life.

THE FALL OF *Caesar*

Judging from the fall in citations and allusions to *Julius Caesar* in the last forty years, it would seem that the play's formerly preeminent brightness in the Shakespearean firmament has decisively waned. The reasons for this shift are many. One is that the grandiloquent public oratory so closely identified with this play has become less appealing in an age of sound bite media and obligatory informal speech. Another, more important reason is that in the seventies *Julius Caesar* began to be required less often in secondary school curricula, replaced by other Shakespearean plays felt to be potentially more relevant to contemporary youth. Perhaps because its subject matter is located in the classical world, the epitome of traditional high culture, *Julius Caesar* has long seemed less amenable to the kind of historical updating and cultural transposition that has become commonplace with other Shakespeare plays.

Indeed, the updating of this particular play is often held up to special ridicule in popular culture, as if it now serves as a quintessential example of the folly of contemporizing Shakespeare. One early example is the classic skit by Canadian comics Wayne and Shuster, "Rinse the Blood Off My Toga," which debuted in 1955 and was performed on *The Ed Sullivan Show* three years later to great acclaim. In this hybrid of Shakespeare and *film noir*, Flavius, a Roman detective, investigates the murder of Julius Caesar, in the process making myriad comic references to all things classical and Roman, including, to take a typical example, "martinus" as the singular for "martini." By stressing the utter incompatibility of allusions, this literate comedy routine lampooned the impulse to bring the classical past into the present. The same mismatch lay behind the Second City comedy routine "Caesar's Wife," a riff on the Wayne and Shuster skit included on their 1961 *Comedy from the Second City* album. Tellingly, both comedy routines are pre-1965, when *Julius Caesar* was still recognizable enough to a wide audience to be the stuff of popular caricature.

This is not to say that *Julius Caesar* has entirely fallen off the radar of youth culture. Teen-market movies still make passing references to it. The films *Killing Mr. Griffin* (1997), *Whatever* (1998), *The Emperor's Club* (2002), and *Mean Girls* (2004) all include classroom scenes that involve the teaching of the play, most with thematic resonances for the remainder of the film. But for most Anglo-American youth *Julius Caesar* has increasingly become a Shakespeare play typical of the conservative or outmoded tastes of their parents and grandparents. Two examples point to the generational divide that now haunts the reputation of *Julius Caesar*. In "Shakespeare," a 1987 episode of *The Cosby Show*, while Theo Huxtable struggles with *Julius Caesar* for a school assignment, his father Cliff and a number of his friends gather for a barbecue. When the conversation turns to Theo's school assignment, the older gentlemen begin to recite passages from the play from memory, a demonstration of their cultural sophistication. When at episode's end Theo reveals the fruits of his studies, he does so with a preposterous *Julius Caesar* rap that his father regards with indulgent bemusement. The show stresses, in other words, the difference between the older generation's knowledge and reverence for *Julius Caesar* and the younger generation's misguided need to translate the play into its own terms.

The film *Free Enterprise* (1998) widens this generational gap. In the film, Mark and Robert, two dysfunctional *Star Trek* fans, encounter their hero William Shatner, star of the TV series, only to discover that he is even more dysfunctional than they are. An important indicator of Shatner's hopeless nerdiness is that he dreams of performing a musical version of *Julius Caesar*, with himself playing all the parts, an idea even more schlocky than the science fiction shows Mark and Robert lionize. At the end of the movie, we are treated to a portion of Shatner's musical, "No Tears for Caesar," a bizarre rap version of Antony's funeral oration performed by Shatner himself in full hip-hop regalia. Once again, the aging Shatner's fluency and reverence for *Julius Caesar* marks him as a member of an older generation, comically unhip no matter how he tries to update his Shakespeare. (Adding to the joke is the fact that Shatner began his career as a promising Shakespearean actor.) And yet despite the fact that the combination of *Julius Caesar* and hip-hop is so often presented as absurd, assimilating the two has persisted as a cultural fantasy.

Caesar AROUND THE WORLD

Though *Julius Caesar*'s status in Western pop culture has demonstrably slipped, the play nonetheless remains a potent resource for other cultures. Like many other Shakespeare plays, *Julius Caesar* has been adapted to a variety of world theatrical styles, including Kabuki theater of Japan (*Kabuki Julius Caesar*, 1997) and Kathakali theater of India (*Kathakali Julius Caesar*, 2005), the latter a tour-de-force with all the parts performed by a single actor. Several African versions, some quite freely adapted, have also been staged, including Rome Neal's *Julius Caesar Set in Africa* (1998), a production that resituates the action to 13th century Mali and Ghana and emphasizes the play's ritual elements through African drumming and dance; Dev Virahsawmy's *Zil Sezar* (1999), a free transposition of the play to the language and setting of Mauritius by the noted intercultural Shakespearean adaptor; and Yael Farber's *SeZaR* (2002), a South African adaptation that combines Shakespeare's text, traditional African motifs, elements from contemporary culture such as rap, and spectacular staging.

GLOBAL JULIUS CAESAR

PRODUCTION	SETTING
Kabuki Julius Caesar (1997)	Kabuki theater of Japan
Julius Caesar Set in Africa (1998)	13th century Mali and Ghana
Zil Sezar (1999)	Mauritius
SeZaR (2002)	South Africa
Kathakali Julius Caesar (2005)	Kathakali theater of India

As Martin Orkin argues in a fascinating study of the play (*Local Shakespeares* [Routledge, 2005], pp. 52–59), Farber's transposition of Shakespeare's play to a different cultural context allows for a reexamination of its basic themes—most notably, male violence and its relationship to state power—from a new perspective, in this case from that of women. By doing so, the play speaks with renewed immediacy to the cycles of political violence that have plagued modern African politics. A similar concern with cultures of violence dominates Malaysian director Namron's *Gedebe* (2002), a work which testifies to the worldwide influence of Baz Luhrmann's youth culture Shakespearean adaptation, *Romeo + Juliet*. *Gedebe* recasts Shakespeare's narrative as a crime drama set in Kuala Lumpur's club subculture, featuring Caesar as a skinhead gang leader and Brutus as an undercover policeman.

These intercultural adaptations remind us that as Shakespeare has gone global in the twentieth century, *Julius Caesar* has become a play that for many is no longer quite so firmly tied to the classical culture of the West and thus may be ripe for popular rediscovery. For a sign of that potential rediscovery, we might look to Antony Johnson and Brett Weldele's *Julius* (2004), a recent graphic novelization of Shakespeare's play that treats the transposition of *Julius Caesar* to urban gangsta culture with respect rather than ridicule.

Dramatis Personae

Caesar (Caius Julius Caesar)

TRIUMVIRS AFTER CAESAR'S DEATH:
Mark Antony (Marcus Antonius)
Octavius (Caius Octavius Caesar)
Lepidus (Marcus Aemilius Lepidus)

CONSPIRATORS AGAINST JULIUS CAESAR:
Brutus (Marcus Junius Brutus)
Cassius (Caius Cassius Longinus)
Casca (Publius Servilius Casca Longus)
Trebonius (Caius Trebonius)
Caius Ligarius (Quintus Ligarius)
Decius Brutus (Decimus Junius Brutus)
Metellus Cimber (Lucius Tillius Cimber)
Cinna (Lucius Cornelius Cinna)

Calphurnia, wife to Caesar
Portia, wife to Brutus

SENATORS:
Cicero (Marcus Tullius Cicero)
Publius
Popilius Lena (Caius Popillius Laenas)

TRIBUNES OF THE PEOPLE:
Flavius (Lucius Caesetius Flavus)
Murellus (Caius Epidius Marullus)

Artemidorus, a teacher of rhetoric
A Soothsayer
Cinna, a poet (Caius Helvius Cinna)
Another poet
Lucius, Brutus's servant

continued on next page

FRIENDS AND SOLDIERS IN BRUTUS'S ARMY:
Lucilius
Titinius
Messala (Marcus Valerius Messala Corvinus)
Young Cato (Marcus Porcius Cato)
Volumnius (Publius Volumnius)
Strato
Varro
Claudius
Clitus
Labeo
Flavius

Caesar's Servant
Antony's Servant
Octavius's Servant
Pindarus (a freed bondman of Cassius)
Dardanius (Brutus's Servant in his army)

A Carpenter
A Cobbler
A Messenger
Senators, Plebeians, Soldiers, and Attendants

Julius Caesar

Act 1

Location: a public place in Rome

Scene: Kemble created a sense of the Citizens' importance in this scene by opening his 1812 production with thirty supernumeraries (minor actors in crowd scenes), a radical change from the eighteenth century practice of using the company's comedians to lead a small cluster of people.

Stage direction: **over the stage:** actors cross the stage before stopping and speaking their lines; since Flavius shouts "Hence!" it seems logical that he and Murellus chase the people some distance across the stage before they start lecturing them

3: **mechanical:** artisan

4: **sign:** (for example, the work clothes and tools that Murellus mentions in line 7)

5: **thou:** the informal, familiar second person pronoun

7: **rule:** ruler for measurement, with a pun on governed behavior

11: **cobbler:** shoemaker, with a pun on bungler

12: **directly:** plainly

14: **soles:** (pun on "souls")

15: **naughty:** worthless

16: **out:** angry; the second "out" is a pun on shoes in disrepair

Act 1, Scene 1]

Enter FLAVIUS, MURELLUS, and
certain Commoners over the stage

FLAVIUS
Hence! Home, you idle creatures, get you home.
Is this a holiday? What, know you not,
Being mechanical, you ought not walk
Upon a laboring day without the sign
Of your profession? Speak, what trade art thou?   5

Carpenter
Why, sir, a carpenter.

MURELLUS
Where is thy leather apron and thy rule?
What dost thou with thy best apparel on?
You, sir, what trade are you?

Cobbler
Truly, sir, in respect of a fine workman, I am but,   10
as you would say, a cobbler.

MURELLUS
But what trade art thou? Answer me directly.

Cobbler
A trade, sir, that, I hope, I may use with a safe conscience, which is,
indeed, sir, a mender of bad soles.

MURELLUS
What trade, thou knave? Thou naughty knave, what trade?   15

Cobbler
Nay, I beseech you, sir, be not out with me. Yet, if you be out, sir,
I can mend you.

19: **cobble:** mend

21: **all that I live by is with the awl:** proverbial, with a sexual pun on the cobbler's awl

21: **meddle:** mix or blend, with sexual innuendo

22: **women's matters:** sexual or romantic affairs

22: **withal:** nevertheless, extending the pun about the cobbler's tool

24: **recover:** shoe repair (with a pun on salvation)

24: **neat's leather:** cowhide

30: **triumph:** Caesar's victory procession through Rome, specifically an October 45 BCE celebration of his defeat of Pompey's sons at Munda, Spain in March that same year

31: "Wherefore rejoice? What conquest brings he home?": John Pieza as Murellus with ensemble in the Shakespeare Theatre of New Jersey's 2005 production directed by Brian B. Crowe

Photo: Gerry Goodstein

31: **conquest:** spoils of war

32: **tributaries:** captives who must pay tribute

33: **captive bonds:** the tributaries' bonds

34: **senseless:** without sensation or intelligence

36: **Pompey:** Gnaeus Pompeius Magnus (106–48 BCE), "the Great." He formed the first triumvirate with Caesar and Crassus, was defeated by Caesar in 48 BCE, and was stabbed to death the same year.

41: **pass the streets:** pass through the streets

MURELLUS
What mean'st thou by that? Mend me, thou saucy fellow!

Cobbler
Why, sir, cobble you.

FLAVIUS
Thou art a cobbler, art thou?   20

Cobbler
Truly, sir, all that I live by is with the awl. I meddle with no
tradesman's matters, nor women's matters, but withal I am
indeed, sir, a surgeon to old shoes: when they are in great danger,
I recover them. As proper men as ever trod upon neat's leather
have gone upon my handiwork.   25

FLAVIUS
But wherefore art not in thy shop today?
Why dost thou lead these men about the streets?

Cobbler
Truly, sir, to wear out their shoes, to get myself into more work.
But indeed, sir, we make holiday to see Caesar and to rejoice in
his triumph.   30

MURELLUS
Wherefore rejoice? What conquest brings he home?
What tributaries follow him to Rome,
To grace in captive bonds his chariot-wheels?
You blocks, you stones, you worse than senseless things!
O you hard hearts, you cruel men of Rome,   35
Knew you not Pompey? Many a time and oft
Have you climbed up to walls and battlements,
To towers and windows, yea, to chimney-tops,
Your infants in your arms, and there have sat
The livelong day, with patient expectation,   40
To see great Pompey pass the streets of Rome.
And when you saw his chariot but appear,
Have you not made an universal shout,

44: **Tiber:** the river that flows through Rome

46: **concave:** hollow

48: **cull out a holiday:** choose a working day and make it a holiday

50: **blood:** both Pompey's literal blood and his sons

52: **intermit:** suspend

57–58: **till the lowest ... of all:** until their tears raise the river to the height of its banks

59: **mettle:** temperament (with a pun on the basest metal in alchemy, lead, which melts or changes easily)

Scene: Along with several others who reviewed Peter Hall's 1995 Royal Shakespeare Company (RSC) production, Peter Holland was unimpressed with the director and his set designer's duplication of this image that hung above the production and the sloppy symbolic purposes to which they later put the image: "John Gunter's set for *Caesar* was a tired recycling of old ideas. I have seen too many productions by now where the stage was dominated by a statue of Caesar. This particular looming head seemed to have been carved out of a giant bar of white chocolate and when the blood ran down it as it hovered over the battlefield of Philippi it looked as though Caesar had a runny nose that needed wiping with a giant tissue."

63: **ceremonies:** ornaments

65: **feast of Lupercal:** celebration of the Roman shepherd god Lupercus

66–73: In the 1953 Mankiewicz film, after Flavius makes this speech and throws down the garlands hanging on Caesar, he tries to leave, but is arrested by a centurion and taken away as am ominous musical theme sounds.

67: **trophies:** the spoils of war mentioned in line 29

67: **about:** move about

68: **vulgar:** the common people

69: **thick:** dense

70–71: **feathers plucked ... ordinary pitch:** in this falconry metaphor, Caesar is likened to the bird of prey who is partially plucked to lower its pitch, the highest point of its flight

72–73: **Who else ... servile fearfulness:** Or else Caesar would sail beyond mortals' vision, like a god, and thus keep them subjugated

That Tiber trembled underneath her banks
To hear the replication of your sounds   45
Made in her concave shores?
And do you now put on your best attire?
And do you now cull out a holiday?
And do you now strew flowers in his way,
That comes in triumph over Pompey's blood? Be gone!   50
Run to your houses, fall upon your knees,
Pray to the gods to intermit the plague
That needs must light on this ingratitude.

FLAVIUS
Go, go, good countrymen, and for this fault
Assemble all the poor men of your sort,   55
Draw them to Tiber banks, and weep your tears
Into the channel, till the lowest stream
Do kiss the most exalted shores of all.

Exeunt all the Commoners

See where their basest mettle be not moved.
They vanish tongue-tied in their guiltiness.   60
Go you down that way towards the Capitol,
This way will I. Disrobe the images
If you do find them decked with ceremonies.

MURELLUS
May we do so?
You know it is the feast of Lupercal.   65

FLAVIUS
It is no matter; let no images
Be hung with Caesar's trophies. I'll about
And drive away the vulgar from the streets;
So do you too, where you perceive them thick.
These growing feathers plucked from Caesar's wing   70
Will make him fly an ordinary pitch,
Who else would soar above the view of men
And keep us all in servile fearfulness.

Exeunt

Location: a public place in Rome

Stage direction: **for the course:** suggests that Antony is dressed for the Lupercalia ceremony, in which young men, dressed only in goatskin loin-cloths, run a course (or race) through the streets, striking any they met with leather strips. The ritual was supposed to cure the sterility of those struck (see 1.2.8–10).

Scene: John Houseman remembers some of the unusual entrances in the 1937 Orson Welles Mercury Theatre production: "Since our stage door opened directly onto the acting area, it was not unusual for people to wander in off the street during performances. . . . Orson himself, arriving late from Longchamp's or Bleeck's, more than once made his entry directly from Forty-first street." Presumably Houseman is referring to Brutus's first entrance since Welles's own cutting only left him thirty-two lines of Antony's speech over Caesar's dead body in 3.2 to step out of and return to the theatre.

2–24:
Harold Gould as Caesar, Jack Coleman as Casca, Bonnie Bedelia as Calphurnia, Richard Dreyfuss as Mark Antony, Basil Langton as Soothsayer, Stacey Keach as Brutus, John de Lancie as Cassius
John Moffat as Caesar, Brian Haines as Casca, Jennie Goossens as Calphurnia, Peter Finch as Mark Antony, Dennis Shaw as Soothsayer, Patrick Wymark as Brutus, Tenniel Evans as Cassius

tracks 2-4

6–7: "Forget not, in your speed, Antonio, / To touch Calphurnia": David McCallum as Julius Caesar and Jeffrey Wright as Mark Antony in the Public Theater's 2000 production directed by Barry Edelstein
Photo: Michal Daniel

Act 1, Scene 2]

Enter CAESAR, ANTONY for the course,
CALPHURNIA, PORTIA, DECIUS, CICERO,
BRUTUS, CASSIUS, CASCA, a SOOTHSAYER,
after them MURELLUS and FLAVIUS

CAESAR
Calphurnia.

CASCA
                Peace ho, Cæsar speaks.

CAESAR
                      Calphurnia.

CALPHURNIA
Here, my lord.

CAESAR
Stand you directly in Antonio's way
When he doth run his course. Antonio.

ANTONY
Caesar, my lord. 5

CAESAR
Forget not, in your speed, Antonio,
To touch Calphurnia, for our elders say
The barren, touched in this holy chase,
Shake off their sterile curse.

ANTONY
               I shall remember.
When Caesar says, "Do this," it is performed. 10

tracks 2-4

2–24:
*Harold Gould as Caesar, Jack Coleman as Casca, Bonnie Bedelia as
Calphurnia, Richard Dreyfuss as Mark Antony, Basil Langton as Soothsayer,
Stacey Keach as Brutus, John de Lancie as Cassius
John Moffat as Caesar, Brian Haines as Casca, Jennie Goossens as Calphurnia,
Peter Finch as Mark Antony, Dennis Shaw as Soothsayer, Patrick Wymark as Brutus,
Tenniel Evans as Cassius*

11: **set on:** begin

14: This line actually opened Welles's production (1937), and was delivered by Caesar.
When he spoke the lines, the ominous music cut out and the lights came up, revealing
the arrogant expression on his face as an offstage voice called "Caesar!"

15: **press:** crowd

18: **Ides of March:** the fifteenth of the month, which is tomorrow in the play

23: "Beware the ides of March": William Metzo as Caesar, Patrick Toon as a Soothsayer,
and ensemble in the Shakespeare Theatre of New Jersey's 2005 production directed by
Brian B. Crowe
Photo: Gerry Goodstein

CAESAR
  Set on, and leave no ceremony out.

SOOTHSAYER
  Caesar!

CAESAR
  Ha? Who calls?

CASCA
  Bid every noise be still. Peace yet again!

CAESAR
  Who is it in the press that calls on me?   15
  I hear a tongue, shriller than all the music
  Cry "Caesar!" Speak. Caesar is turned to hear.

SOOTHSAYER
  Beware the Ides of March.

CAESAR
                    What man is that?

BRUTUS
  A soothsayer bids you beware the Ides of March.

CAESAR
  Set him before me; let me see his face.   20

CASSIUS
  Fellow, come from the throng, look upon Caesar.

CAESAR
  What say'st thou to me now? Speak once again.

SOOTHSAYER
  Beware the ides of March.

24: After Caesar dismissed the offstage speaker in Welles's production (1937), the crowd called "Hail Caesar!" raising their arms in a fascist salute while the menacing rhythms of numerous marching feet were heard.

24: **dreamer:** one who has visions

24: **pass:** proceed

Stage direction: **sennet:** set of notes played on the trumpet or cornet

25–177: Kemble (1812) had Brutus and Cassius speak these lines well downstage, and their proximity to the audience allowed a more intimate tone between the two actors. This intimacy stood in sharp contrast to the pomp that attended the exit (1.2.24), reentry (1.2.177), and second exit (1.2.214) of Caesar's huge procession, which included priests, senators, maidens, lectors, guards, and gold and silver eagles on standards, in addition to the principal actors.

28: **gamesome:** interested in sport, perhaps with a pun on frivolous

29: **quick:** fast, but also lively

34: **wont:** accustomed, used

34: **strange:** unfriendly, unfamiliar

37–39: **If I . . . upon myself:** If I have been remote, it is to keep my worries private

40: **passions of some difference:** conflicting emotions

41: **conceptions . . . myself:** thoughts concerning only me

42: **soil:** stain, blemish

CAESAR
    He is a dreamer; let us leave him. Pass.
                    Sennet. Exeunt. Manet BRUTUS and CASSIUS.

CASSIUS
    Will you go see the order of the course?   25

BRUTUS
    Not I.

CASSIUS
    I pray you do.

BRUTUS
    I am not gamesome; I do lack some part
    Of that quick spirit that is in Antony.
    Let me not hinder, Cassius, your desires;   30
    I'll leave you.

CASSIUS
    Brutus, I do observe you now of late.
    I have not from your eyes that gentleness
    And show of love as I was wont to have.
    You bear too stubborn and too strange a hand   35
    Over your friend that loves you.

BRUTUS
                    Cassius,
    Be not deceived. If I have veiled my look,
    I turn the trouble of my countenance
    Merely upon myself. Vexed I am
    Of late with passions of some difference,   40
    Conceptions only proper to myself,
    Which give some soil, perhaps, to my behaviors.
    But let not therefore my good friends be grieved—
    Among which number, Cassius, be you one—
    Nor construe any further my neglect,   45
    Than that poor Brutus, with himself at war,
    Forgets the shows of love to other men.

50: **cogitations:** thoughts

58: **shadow:** reflection

59: **the best respect in Rome:** the most respected, highest ranking Romans

60: **immortal:** (meant ironically)

62: **his eyes:** either the speaker's eyes, or that Brutus could accurately see Caesar's tyranny

66: **therefore:** as for that

68: **glass:** mirror

69: **modestly discover:** reflect without exaggeration

71: **jealous on:** suspicious of

72: **common laugher:** one not taken seriously; a laughingstock

73–74: **To stale . . . new protester:** to cheapen the professed friendship of new acquaintances with common oaths or declarations

76: **scandal:** libel, slander

77: **profess myself:** profess friendship

77: **banqueting:** feasting

78: **rout:** rabble

Stage direction: **flourish:** fanfare for persons of high rank

CASSIUS

    Then, Brutus, I have much mistook your passion,
    By means whereof this breast of mine hath buried
    Thoughts of great value, worthy cogitations.   50
    Tell me, good Brutus, can you see your face?

BRUTUS

    No, Cassius, for the eye sees not itself,
    But by reflection, by some other things.

CASSIUS

    'Tis just,
    And it is very much lamented, Brutus,   55
    That you have no such mirrors as will turn
    Your hidden worthiness into your eye
    That you might see your shadow. I have heard
    Where many of the best respect in Rome—
    Except immortal Caesar—speaking of Brutus,   60
    And groaning underneath this age's yoke,
    Have wished that noble Brutus had his eyes.

BRUTUS

    Into what dangers would you lead me, Cassius,
    That you would have me seek into myself
    For that which is not in me?   65

CASSIUS

    Therefore, good Brutus, be prepared to hear.
    And since you know you cannot see yourself
    So well as by reflection, I, your glass,
    Will modestly discover to yourself
    That of yourself which you yet know not of.   70
    And be not jealous on me, gentle Brutus.
    Were I a common laugher, or did use
    To stale with ordinary oaths my love
    To every new protester; if you know
    That I do fawn on men, and hug them hard   75
    And after scandal them, or if you know
    That I profess myself in banqueting
    To all the rout, then hold me dangerous.

                                     Flourish and shout

79: In an unusual choice, Peter Hall (1995, RSC) had Caesar's procession exit into a trap door in the stage floor, allowing light to pour out from under the platform onto the half-lit stage. In her review, Jean-Marie Maguin wrote of the staging of the scene: "The vivid lighting, contrasting with the dusk in which Brutus and Cassius are talking, helps focus Brutus's attention and our own onto the all-important event which takes place out of sight: the offering of a crown to Caesar by Mark Antony. The noise of the people shouting, which erupts from under the stage platform draws the two men towards the pool of light which Brutus anxiously peers into."

80–81: "Ay, do you fear it? / Then must I think you would not have it so": John Gielgud as Cassius and James Mason as Brutus in the 1953 movie directed by Joseph Mankiewicz

© Sunset Boulevard/ CORBIS Sygma

85: **aught:** anything
87: **indifferently:** with indifference or impartially
91: **outward favor:** appearance
95: **lief:** soon
101: **chafing:** colliding roughly against
105: **accoutred:** dressed
107: **buffet:** beat
108: **lusty sinews:** i.e., strength, vigor
109: **stemming:** pushing through
109: **hearts of controversy:** eager to contend against the waves

BRUTUS
>What means this shouting? I do fear, the people
>Choose Caesar for their king.

CASSIUS
>   Ay, do you fear it?   80
>Then must I think you would not have it so.

BRUTUS
>I would not, Cassius, yet I love him well.
>But wherefore do you hold me here so long?
>What is it that you would impart to me?
>If it be aught toward the general good,   85
>Set honor in one eye and death i' th' other,
>And I will look on both indifferently.
>For let the gods so speed me as I love
>The name of honor more than I fear death.

CASSIUS
>I know that virtue to be in you, Brutus,   90
>As well as I do know your outward favor.
>Well, honor is the subject of my story.
>I cannot tell what you and other men
>Think of this life, but, for my single self,
>I had as lief not be as live to be   95
>In awe of such a thing as I myself.
>I was born free as Caesar; so were you;
>We both have fed as well, and we can both
>Endure the winter's cold as well as he.
>For once, upon a raw and gusty day,   100
>The troubled Tiber, chafing with her shores,
>Caesar said to me "Dar'st thou, Cassius, now
>Leap in with me into this angry flood,
>And swim to yonder point?" Upon the word,
>Accoutred as I was, I plungèd in   105
>And bade him follow; so indeed he did.
>The torrent roared, and we did buffet it
>With lusty sinews, throwing it aside
>And stemming it with hearts of controversy.

110: **ere:** before

112–114: **Aeneas ... Anchises bear:** in Virgil's *Aeneid*, Aeneas rescues his father, Anchises, from Troy as the Greeks burn it. Aeneas later founded Rome.

117: **bend:** bow

123: **bend:** gaze, look

124: **his:** its

129: **temper:** (also temperament)

130–131: **get the start ... bear the palm:** either be positioned advantageously within a pack of runners or outstrip the others in a race and thus win the palm as a sign of victory

135: **bestride:** straddle

Set rendering from the May 28, 1957, staging by the Royal Shakespeare Company at the Shakespeare Memorial Theatre directed by Glen Byam Shaw

Rare Book and Special Collections Library, University of Illinois at Urbana-Champaign

136: **Colossus:** a giant statue, likely the huge statue of Apollo at Rhodes, which, at a reported 100 feet, was said to straddle the harbor and was one of the seven wonders of the world

140: **stars:** (refers to the belief that people's lives and characters are governed by astrological forces)

141: **underlings:** persons of low birth

But ere we could arrive the point proposed,   110
Caesar cried, "Help me, Cassius, or I sink!"
I, as Aeneas, our great ancestor,
Did from the flames of Troy upon his shoulder
The old Anchises bear, so from the waves of Tiber
Did I the tired Caesar. And this man   115
Is now become a god, and Cassius is
A wretched creature and must bend his body,
If Caesar carelessly but nod on him.
He had a fever when he was in Spain,
And when the fit was on him, I did mark   120
How he did shake. 'Tis true, this god did shake,
His coward lips did from their color fly,
And that same eye, whose bend doth awe the world,
Did lose his luster. I did hear him groan.
Ay, and that tongue of his, that bade the Romans   125
Mark him and write his speeches in their books,
"Alas," it cried, "Give me some drink, Titinius,"
As a sick girl. Ye gods, it doth amaze me
A man of such a feeble temper should
So get the start of the majestic world   130
And bear the palm alone.
                                                    Shout. Flourish.

BRUTUS
Another general shout?
I do believe that these applauses are
For some new honors that are heaped on Caesar.

CASSIUS
Why, man, he doth bestride the narrow world   135
Like a Colossus, and we petty men
Walk under his huge legs and peep about
To find ourselves dishonorable graves.
Men at some time are masters of their fates.
The fault, dear Brutus, is not in our stars,   140
But in ourselves, that we are underlings.
"Brutus" and "Caesar." What should be in that "Caesar?"
Why should that name be sounded more than yours?

146: **conjure:** speak the names like spells to raise spirits or the dead

147: **start:** raise

151: **breed of noble bloods:** bloodline of those of noble rank

152: **great flood:** (in Greek mythology, Zeus flooded the world to punish humanity for its sins)

153: **famed with:** renowned for

155: **walks:** tracts of land

156: **Rome indeed and room:** (a pun, as the words were homophones in Elizabethan English)

159: **Brutus:** Lucius Junius Brutus, who helped expel the Tarquins from Rome, became one of the first two Consuls in the Roman republic in the sixth century BCE

159: **brooked:** withstood, tolerated

162: **nothing jealous:** not mistrustful

163: **work:** convince, persuade

163: **aim:** guess, notion

166: **so with love I might entreat you:** if I might ask you out of our friendship

170: **meet:** appropriate

170: **high:** exalted

171: **chew upon:** consider

173: **repute:** esteem

177: "I am glad that my weak words / Have struck but thus much show of fire from Brutus": Patrick Stewart as Cassius and John Wood as Brutus in the Royal Shakespeare Company's 1972 production directed by Trevor Nunn

© Royal Shakespeare Company

Stage direction: **train:** attendants

Write them together, yours is as fair a name.
Sound them, it doth become the mouth as well.   145
Weigh them, it is as heavy; conjure with 'em.
Brutus will start a spirit as soon as Caesar.
Now in the names of all the gods at once,
Upon what meat doth this our Caesar feed
That he is grown so great? Age, thou art shamed!   150
Rome, thou hast lost the breed of noble bloods!
When went there by an age since the great flood
But it was famed with more than with one man?
When could they say, till now, that talked of Rome,
That her wide walks encompassed but one man?   155
Now is it Rome indeed and room enough,
When there is in it but one only man.
O, you and I have heard our fathers say,
There was a Brutus once that would have brooked
Th' eternal devil to keep his state in Rome   160
As easily as a king.

BRUTUS

That you do love me, I am nothing jealous;
What you would work me to, I have some aim.
How I have thought of this and of these times,
I shall recount hereafter. For this present,   165
I would not, so with love I might entreat you,
Be any further moved. What you have said
I will consider; what you have to say
I will with patience hear and find a time
Both meet to hear and answer such high things.   170
Till then, my noble friend, chew upon this:
Brutus had rather be a villager
Than to repute himself a son of Rome
Under these hard conditions as this time
Is like to lay upon us.   175

CASSIUS

I am glad that my weak words
Have struck but thus much show of fire from Brutus.

                              Enter CAESAR and his TRAIN

186: **ferret:** red (with anger)

188: **crossed:** opposed

188: **conference:** debate

193: **sleek-headed:** unworried

194: "Yond Cassius has a lean and hungry look": Earl Hindman as Julius Caesar and Graham Winton as Mark Antony in Theater for a New Audience's 2003 production directed by Karin Coonrod
Photo: Gerry Goodstein

197: **well given:** well-disposed

199: **if my name were liable to fear:** Caesar suggests that his title protects him and thus, he has nothing to fear

BRUTUS
    The games are done and Caesar is returning.

CASSIUS
    As they pass by, pluck Casca by the sleeve
    And he will, after his sour fashion, tell you   180
    What hath proceeded worthy note today.

BRUTUS
    I will do so. But, look you, Cassius,
    The angry spot doth glow on Caesar's brow,
    And all the rest look like a chidden train.
    Calphurnia's cheek is pale, and Cicero   185
    Looks with such ferret and such fiery eyes
    As we have seen him in the Capitol,
    Being crossed in conference by some senators.

CASSIUS
    Casca will tell us what the matter is.

CAESAR
    Antonio.   190

ANTONY
    Caesar.

CAESAR
    Let me have men about me that are fat,
    Sleek-headed men and such as sleep a-nights.
    Yond Cassius has a lean and hungry look,
    He thinks too much; such men are dangerous.   195

ANTONY
    Fear him not, Caesar; he's not dangerous,
    He is a noble Roman and well given.

CAESAR
    Would he were fatter! But I fear him not.
    Yet if my name were liable to fear,

202–203: looks quite through the deeds of men: perceives hidden motives

203–204: "He loves no plays, / As thou dost, Antony": William Metzo as Julius Caesar and Gregory Derelian as Mark Antony in the Shakespeare Theatre of New Jersey's 2005 production directed by Brian B. Crowe

Photo: Gerry Goodstein

204: hears no music: (Caesar equates Cassius's austere disregard of pleasure with a calculating and restless nature)

205: sort: way, fashion

212: Welles closed the scene at "for always I am Caesar" with a dramatic use of light and sound that characterized the production: thunder rolled, the lights washed out with a burst of lightning, and a second burst revealed the empty stage.

213: deaf: (Caesar's deafness is Shakespeare's invention)

216: chanced: happened, occurred

217: sad: serious

221: put it by: refused it (the crown)

I do not know the man I should avoid   200
So soon as that spare Cassius. He reads much,
He is a great observer, and he looks
Quite through the deeds of men. He loves no plays,
As thou dost, Antony, he hears no music;
Seldom he smiles, and smiles in such a sort   205
As if he mocked himself and scorned his spirit
That could be moved to smile at anything.
Such men as he be never at heart's ease
Whiles they behold a greater than themselves,
And therefore are they very dangerous.   210
I rather tell thee what is to be feared
Than what I fear, for always I am Caesar.
Come on my right hand, for this ear is deaf,
And tell me truly what thou think'st of him.
                    Sennet. Exeunt CAESAR and his TRAIN.

CASCA
    You pulled me by the cloak, would you speak with me?   215

BRUTUS
    Ay, Casca, tell us what hath chanced today
    That Caesar looks so sad.

CASCA
    Why, you were with him, were you not?

BRUTUS
    I should not then ask Casca what had chanced.

CASCA
    Why, there was a crown offered him, and being offered him, he   220
    put it by with the back of his hand, thus, and then the people fell
    a-shouting.

BRUTUS
    What was the second noise for?

CASCA
    Why, for that too.

228–229: **gentler than other:** with greater reluctance

232: **gentle:** noble

233: "I can as well be hanged as tell the manner of it": Roscoe Orman as Brutus, Morgan Freeman as Casca, and Gylan Cain as Cassius in the Public Theater's 1979 production directed by Michael Langham
Photo: George E. Joseph

235: **coronets:** small crowns

237: **fain:** gladly

241: **chapped:** roughened

244: **swounded:** swooned

246: **swound:** swoon

CASSIUS

They shouted thrice. What was the last cry for?   225

CASCA

Why, for that too.

BRUTUS

Was the crown offered him thrice?

CASCA

Ay, marry, was't, and he put it by thrice, every time gentler than other, and at every putting-by, mine honest neighbors shouted.

CASSIUS

Who offered him the crown?   230

CASCA

Why, Antony.

BRUTUS

Tell us the manner of it, gentle Casca.

CASCA

I can as well be hanged as tell the manner of it. It was mere foolery; I did not mark it. I saw Mark Antony offer him a crown— yet 'twas not a crown neither, 'twas one of these coronets—and,   235 as I told you, he put it by once, but, for all that, to my thinking, he would fain have had it. Then he offered it to him again; then he put it by again, but, to my thinking, he was very loath to lay his fingers off it. And then he offered it the third time; he put it the third time by, and still as he refused it, the rabblement hooted   240 and clapped their chapped hands and threw up their sweaty nightcaps and uttered such a deal of stinking breath because Caesar refused the crown that it had almost choked Caesar, for he swounded and fell down at it. And for mine own part, I durst not laugh, for fear of opening my lips and receiving the bad air.   245

CASSIUS

But soft, I pray you, what, did Caesar swound?

249: **like:** likely

249: **falling sickness:** epilepsy

251: **falling sickness:** Cassius is alluding to the much lower stature of Brutus, Casca, and himself

253: **tag-rag people:** rabble

256: **unto himself:** to consciousness

258–259: "He plucked me ope his doublet and / offered them his throat to cut": Charles Durning as Casca with ensemble in the Public Theater's 1962 production directed by Joseph Papp

Photo: George E. Joseph

258: **plucked me ope:** opened

258: **doublet:** a short jacket

259: **an:** if

266: **stabbed:** possibly a bawdy pun for sexual penetration

CASCA

He fell down in the marketplace, and foamed at mouth, and was
speechless.

BRUTUS

'Tis very like, he hath the falling sickness.

CASSIUS

No, Caesar hath it not, but you and I,   250
And honest Casca, we have the falling sickness.

CASCA

I know not what you mean by that, but, I am sure, Caesar fell down.
If the tag-rag people did not clap him and hiss him, according as he
pleased and displeased them, as they use to do the players in the
theatre, I am no true man.   255

BRUTUS

What said he when he came unto himself?

CASCA

Marry, before he fell down, when he perceived the common herd
was glad he refused the crown, he plucked me ope his doublet and
offered them his throat to cut. An I had been a man of any
occupation, if I would not have taken him at a word, I would I   260
might go to hell among the rogues. And so he fell. When he came
to himself again, he said if he had done or said anything amiss, he
desired their worships to think it was his infirmity. Three or four
wenches, where I stood, cried, "Alas, good soul!" and forgave him
with all their hearts. But there's no heed to be taken of them. If   265
Caesar had stabbed their mothers, they would have done no less.

BRUTUS

And after that, he came thus sad away?

CASCA

Ay.

272: "Nay, an I tell you that, I'll ne'er look you i' th' face again": Robert Cuccioli as Brutus, Richard Topol as Cassius, and Leon Addison Brown as Casca in the Shakespeare Theatre of New Jersey's 2005 production directed by Brian B. Crowe
Photo: Gerry Goodstein

279: **promised forth:** already engaged

281: **your mind hold:** you don't change your mind

286: **quick mettle:** lively, spirited

CASSIUS
Did Cicero say anything?

CASCA
Ay, he spoke Greek.   270

CASSIUS
To what effect?

CASCA
Nay, an I tell you that, I'll ne'er look you i' th' face again. But
those that understood him smiled at one another and shook their
heads; but, for mine own part, it was Greek to me. I could tell you
more news too: Murellus and Flavius, for pulling scarves off   275
Caesar's images, are put to silence. Fare you well. There was
more foolery yet, if I could remember it.

CASSIUS
Will you sup with me tonight, Casca?

CASCA
No, I am promised forth.

CASSIUS
Will you dine with me tomorrow?   280

CASCA
Ay, if I be alive, and your mind hold, and your dinner worth the
eating.

CASSIUS
Good, I will expect you.

CASCA
Do so. Farewell, both.

Exit CASCA

BRUTUS
What a blunt fellow is this grown to be!   285
He was quick mettle when he went to school.

289: **tardy form:** pretense of slow-wittedness
290: **rudeness:** bluntness, rough manner
297: **the world:** the state of affairs in Rome

298–312:
Orson Welles as Cassius
John de Lancie as Cassius

tracks 5-7

299–300: **wrought from that is disposed:** worked on and turned from its natural disposition
300: **meet:** fitting
303: **bear me hard:** bear me ill will, or endure me very reluctantly
305: **humor:** influence
306: **several hands:** in different handwritings
309: **obscurely:** cryptically
310: **glancèd at:** hinted
311: **seat him sure:** secure himself
301–1.3.13: Mankiewicz's 1953 film created a powerful sense of impending doom between the end of Cassius's speech here and the first exchange between Cicero and Casca. Gielgud as Cassius walks out of the piazza where the preceding action took place, having spoken his final lines with great drama. The camera remains focused on the statue and monument-filled square, and as menacing music builds, the wind picks up and thunder cracks. The film then cuts to a darkened sky broken by a set of stairs, which Casca descends. With his knife drawn and a fearful look on his face, Casca spies three figures crossing the square. As he ducks behind an archway, lightning flashes, revealing Gielgud's watchful Cassius who also descends to eavesdrop around the corner. A *film noir* aura of paranoia pervades the next scene as Mankiewicz shoots all the characters against doorways, archways and walls that hedge them in and shroud them in semi-darkness.

CASSIUS
> So is he now in execution
> Of any bold or noble enterprise,
> However he puts on this tardy form.
> This rudeness is a sauce to his good wit,   290
> Which gives men stomach to digest his words
> With better appetite.

BRUTUS
> And so it is. For this time I will leave you.
> Tomorrow, if you please to speak with me,
> I will come home to you; or, if you will,   295
> Come home to me and I will wait for you.

CASSIUS
> I will do so. Till then, think of the world.

Exit BRUTUS

> Well, Brutus, thou art noble; yet, I see
> Thy honorable mettle may be wrought
> From that it is disposed. Therefore it is meet   300
> That noble minds keep ever with their likes,
> For who so firm that cannot be seduced?
> Caesar doth bear me hard, but he loves Brutus.
> If I were Brutus now and he were Cassius,
> He should not humor me. I will this night,   305
> In several hands, in at his windows throw,
> As if they came from several citizens,
> Writings all tending to the great opinion
> That Rome holds of his name, wherein obscurely
> Caesar's ambition shall be glancèd at.   310
> And after this let Caesar seat him sure,
> For we will shake him, or worse days endure.

Exit

Location: a street in Rome

3: **all the sway of earth:** everything in the world

6: **rived:** split

8: **exalted with:** raised to the level of

12: **saucy:** insolent

18: **sensible of:** feeling the effects of

20: **against:** by, next to

21: **glazed:** stared

21: **surly:** morosely

22: **annoying:** harming, injuring

22–23: **drawn upon a heap:** gathered closely together

23: **ghastly:** pale and fearful

Thunder and lightning. Enter CASCA and CICERO.

CICERO

    Good even, Casca, brought you Caesar home?
    Why are you breathless, and why stare you so?

CASCA

    Are not you moved, when all the sway of earth
    Shakes like a thing unfirm? O Cicero,
    I have seen tempests when the scolding winds   5
    Have rived the knotty oaks, and I have seen
    Th' ambitious ocean swell, and rage, and foam,
    To be exalted with the threatening clouds;
    But never till tonight, never till now,
    Did I go through a tempest dropping fire.   10
    Either there is a civil strife in heaven,
    Or else the world, too saucy with the gods,
    Incenses them to send destruction.

CICERO

    Why, saw you anything more wonderful?

CASCA

    A common slave—you know him well by sight—   15
    Held up his left hand, which did flame and burn
    Like twenty torches joined, and yet his hand,
    Not sensible of fire, remained unscorched.
    Besides—I ha' not since put up my sword—
    Against the Capitol I met a lion,   20
    Who glazed upon me and went surly by
    Without annoying me. And there were drawn
    Upon a heap a hundred ghastly women,
    Transformèd with their fear, who swore they saw
    Men, all in fire, walk up and down the streets.   25

26: **bird of night:** screech-owl, a bird of ill omen

28: **prodigies:** omens

29: **conjointly meet:** occur at once

32: **climate:** region

33: **strange-disposèd:** exceptionally unsettled

34: **after their fashion:** in their own manner

35: **clean from:** far from

33: "Indeed, it is a strange-disposèd time": Jason Novak as Popilius Lena, Emery Battis as Cicero, and Eric Hoffman as Casca in the Shakespeare Theatre Company's 1993–94 production directed by Joe Dowling
Photo: Richard Anderson

And yesterday the bird of night did sit
Even at noon-day upon the market-place,
Hooting and shrieking. When these prodigies
Do so conjointly meet, let not men say
"These are their reasons; they are natural," 30
For I believe they are portentous things
Unto the climate that they point upon.

CICERO

Indeed, it is a strange-disposèd time.
But men may construe things after their fashion,
Clean from the purpose of the things themselves. 35
Comes Caesar to the Capitol tomorrow?

CASCA

He doth, for he did bid Antonio
Send word to you he would be there tomorrow.

CICERO

Good night then, Casca. This disturbèd sky
Is not to walk in.

CASCA

                              Farewell, Cicero. 40

                              Exit CICERO. Enter CASSIUS.

CASSIUS

Who's there?

CASCA

                    A Roman.

CASSIUS

                              Casca, by your voice.

CASCA

Your ear is good. Cassius, what night is this?

CASSIUS

A very pleasing night to honest men.

48: **unbracèd:** with doublet open or undone
49: **thunder-stone:** thunderbolt
50: **cross:** forked
52: **even:** directly
56: **astonish:** scare, stun

57–59: "You are dull, Casca, and those sparks of life / That should be in a Roman you do want, / Or else you use not": Eric Hoffmann as Casca and Philip Goodwin as Cassius in the Shakespeare Theatre Company's 1993–94 production directed by Joe Dowling
Photo: Richard Anderson

57: **dull:** dull-witted
58: **want:** lack
60: **put on:** make an outward show of
60: **wonder:** amazement, astonishment
64: **from quality and kind:** opposite to their nature
65: **old men, fools, and children calculate:** Cassius suggests that there are so many omens that even the very old, fools, and the very young can easily interpret their meanings
66: **ordinance:** their nature as ordained by Providence
67: **preformèd:** innate
68: **monstrous:** unnatural

CASCA
> Who ever knew the heavens menace so?

CASSIUS
> Those that have known the earth so full of faults.   45
> For my part, I have walked about the streets,
> Submitting me unto the perilous night,
> And, thus unbracèd, Casca, as you see,
> Have bared my bosom to the thunder-stone;
> And when the cross blue lightning seemed to open   50
> The breast of heaven, I did present myself
> Even in the aim and very flash of it.

CASCA
> But wherefore did you so much tempt the heavens?
> It is the part of men to fear and tremble,
> When the most mighty gods by tokens send   55
> Such dreadful heralds to astonish us.

CASSIUS
> You are dull, Casca, and those sparks of life
> That should be in a Roman you do want,
> Or else you use not. You look pale and gaze
> And put on fear and cast yourself in wonder   60
> To see the strange impatience of the heavens.
> But if you would consider the true cause
> Why all these fires, why all these gliding ghosts,
> Why birds and beasts from quality and kind,
> Why old men, fools, and children calculate,   65
> Why all these things change from their ordinance,
> Their natures and preformèd faculties
> To monstrous quality, why, you shall find
> That heaven hath infused them with these spirits
> To make them instruments of fear and warning   70
> Unto some monstrous state.
> Now could I, Casca, name to thee a man
> Most like this dreadful night,
> That thunders, lightens, opens graves, and roars
> As doth the lion in the Capitol,   75

77: **prodigious:** monstrous, menacing

78: **fearful:** terrifying

81: **thews:** sinews

82: **woe the while:** alas for the times

84: **yoke and sufferance:** servitude and endurance

91: **therein:** (through suicide)

93: **nor:** neither

95: **be retentive to:** keep imprisoned

97: **dismiss:** end, destroy

98: **know all the world besides:** let the rest of the world know

102: **cancel:** a legal term for annulling a contract

A man no mightier than thyself or me
In personal action, yet prodigious grown
And fearful, as these strange eruptions are.

CASCA

'Tis Caesar that you mean, is it not, Cassius?

CASSIUS

Let it be who it is, for Romans now   80
Have thews and limbs like to their ancestors;
But, woe the while, our fathers' minds are dead,
And we are governed with our mothers' spirits;
Our yoke and sufferance show us womanish.

CASCA

Indeed, they say the senators tomorrow   85
Mean to establish Caesar as a king,
And he shall wear his crown by sea and land,
In every place, save here in Italy.

CASSIUS

I know where I will wear this dagger then;
Cassius from bondage will deliver Cassius.   90
Therein, ye gods, you make the weak most strong;
Therein, ye gods, you tyrants do defeat.
Nor stony tower, nor walls of beaten brass,
Nor airless dungeon, nor strong links of iron,
Can be retentive to the strength of spirit;   95
But life, being weary of these worldly bars,
Never lacks power to dismiss itself.
If I know this, know all the world besides,
That part of tyranny that I do bear
I can shake off at pleasure.

Thunder

CASCA

                    So can I,   100
So every bondman in his own hand bears
The power to cancel his captivity.

106: **hinds:** deer, with a pun on servant

108: **trash:** twigs

109: **rubbish:** debris

109: **offal:** wood chips

110: **base matter:** kindling

111: **vile:** without worth

113: **bondman:** slave

114: **my answer must be made:** I must answer, or pay, for my words

115: **indifferent:** negligible, unimportant

117: **fleering:** sneering

117: **my hand:** here is my hand

118: **be factious:** organize a faction

118: **griefs:** grievances

119–120: **I will . . . goes farthest:** I will go as far as any member of the faction

123: **undergo:** undertake

125: **stay:** wait

126: **Pompey's porch:** a porch adjacent to Pompey's Theatre built in 55 BCE, and the place of Caesar's assassination in Plutarch (Shakespeare's primary source for this play is Plutarch's *The Lives of Noble Grecians and Romans*, translated from the French by Sir Thomas North in 1579).

128: **complexion of the element:** disposition and appearance of the heavens or skies

129: **favor's like:** appearance similar to

CASSIUS

And why should Caesar be a tyrant then?
Poor man, I know he would not be a wolf,
But that he sees the Romans are but sheep.   105
He were no lion, were not Romans hinds.
Those that with haste will make a mighty fire
Begin it with weak straws. What trash is Rome,
What rubbish and what offal, when it serves
For the base matter to illuminate   110
So vile a thing as Caesar? But, O grief,
Where hast thou led me? I perhaps speak this
Before a willing bondman, then I know
My answer must be made. But I am armed,
And dangers are to me indifferent.   115

CASCA

You speak to Casca, and to such a man
That is no fleering telltale. Hold, my hand.
Be factious for redress of all these griefs,
And I will set this foot of mine as far
As who goes farthest.

CASSIUS

                    There's a bargain made.   120
Now know you, Casca, I have moved already
Some certain of the noblest-minded Romans
To undergo with me an enterprise
Of honorable dangerous consequence.
And I do know by this they stay for me   125
In Pompey's porch. For now, this fearful night,
There is no stir or walking in the streets,
And the complexion of the element
In favor's like the work we have in hand,
Most bloody, fiery, and most terrible.   130

Enter CINNA

131: **close:** hidden

135–136: **incorporate to:** in league with

142: **be you content:** do not worry

142–143: "Good Cinna, take this paper / And look you lay it in the praetor's chair": Tristan Colton as Cinna and Richard Topol as Cassius in the Shakespeare Theatre of New Jersey's 2005 production directed by Brian B. Crowe
Photo: Gerry Goodstein

143: **praetor:** chief Roman magistrate (Caesar made Brutus praetor in 44 BCE)

144: **may but:** will certainly

147: **repair:** go

148: **Decius Brutus:** actually Decimus Brutus, who was very favorably treated by Caesar

150: **hie:** go quickly

CASCA
Stand close awhile, for here comes one in haste.

CASSIUS
'Tis Cinna; I do know him by his gait;
He is a friend. Cinna, where haste you so?

CINNA
To find out you. Who's that? Metellus Cimber?

CASSIUS
No, it is Casca; one incorporate   135
To our attempts. Am I not stayed for, Cinna?

CINNA
I am glad on 't. What a fearful night is this!
There's two or three of us have seen strange sights.

CASSIUS
Am I not stayed for? Tell me.

CINNA
                    Yes, you are.
O Cassius, if you could   140
But win the noble Brutus to our party—

CASSIUS
Be you content. Good Cinna, take this paper
And look you lay it in the praetor's chair,
Where Brutus may but find it; and throw this
In at his window; set this up with wax   145
Upon old Brutus' statue. All this done,
Repair to Pompey's porch, where you shall find us.
Is Decius Brutus and Trebonius there?

CINNA
All but Metellus Cimber; and he's gone
To seek you at your house. Well, I will hie,   150
And so bestow these papers as you bade me.

154–155: "Three parts of him / Is ours already": Simeon Moore as Casca and Daniel Oreskes as Cassius in Theater for a New Audience's 2003 production directed by Karin Coonrod

Photo: Gerry Goodstein

156: **yields him ours:** makes him part of our conspiracy

159: **countenance:** appearance, disposition

159–160: **alchemy will . . . to worthiness:** Brutus's involvement in the plot will turn base motives into noble ones, just as alchemists turned base metals into precious ones

162: **conceited:** understood, conceived

CASSIUS

That done, repair to Pompey's theatre.

Exit CINNA

Come, Casca, you and I will yet, ere day,
See Brutus at his house. Three parts of him
Is ours already, and the man entire   155
Upon the next encounter yields him ours.

CASCA

O, he sits high in all the people's hearts,
And that which would appear offense in us,
His countenance, like richest alchemy,
Will change to virtue and to worthiness.   160

CASSIUS

Him and his worth and our great need of him
You have right well conceited. Let us go,
For it is after midnight, and ere day
We will awake him and be sure of him.

Exeunt

[Julius Caesar

Act 2

Stage direction: **orchard:** this is the only location specifically indicated in the Folio
Stage direction: **orchard:** garden

Scene: Welles's lighting designer, Jean Rosenthal, describes the role that chance played in devising one of the 1937 production's many evocative lighting effects: "During a dress rehearsal someone forgot to turn out the bald overhead work lights—whose sole purpose is to illuminate the grid from which the scenery ropes and pulleys are suspended—and they continued to shine down during the blackout just before the orchard scene. The pattern, crisscrossing the stage, conveyed an impression of ground beneath bare branches. Paradoxically in view of the hard planning and thinking I believe in, accident is often the source of inspiration."

2: **progress of the stars:** the stars' positions in the sky
5: **when, Lucius, when:** expression of impatience
7: **taper:** candle

Scene: Mankiewicz achieved a lighting effect similar to Welles's in his 1953 film by having James Mason's Brutus stand under the shadows cast by overhanging branches as he delivered his speech. The effect of the lighting was to make Brutus seem entangled in the web of political intrigue that he and Cassius were about to spin.

10–27:
Introduction to Speaking Shakespeare: Derek Jacobi
Speaking Shakespeare: Andrew Wade with Drew Cortese

10: **his:** Caesar's
11: **spurn:** kick violently
12: **general:** common good
14: **It is the bright day that brings forth the adder:** (proverbial) good can bring about evil
15: **craves:** requires
15: **crown him that:** either make him king or an adder or both
16: **put a sting in him:** i.e., make him dangerous
17: **danger:** harm, damage
18: **disjoins:** separates
19: **remorse:** compassion
20: **affections:** passions, emotions
20: **swayed:** ruled (his behavior)
21: **proof:** experience

tracks 46-47

Act 2, Scene 1]

Enter BRUTUS in his orchard

BRUTUS
What, Lucius, ho!
I cannot, by the progress of the stars,
Give guess how near to day. Lucius, I say!
I would it were my fault to sleep so soundly.
When, Lucius, when? Awake, I say! What, Lucius!   5

Enter LUCIUS

LUCIUS
Called you, my lord?

BRUTUS
Get me a taper in my study, Lucius.
When it is lighted, come and call me here.

LUCIUS
I will, my lord.

Exit

BRUTUS
It must be by his death. And for my part,   10
I know no personal cause to spurn at him,
But for the general. He would be crowned:
How that might change his nature, there's the question.
It is the bright day that brings forth the adder
And that craves wary walking. Crown him that,   15
And then I grant we put a sting in him,
That at his will he may do danger with.
Th'abuse of greatness is when it disjoins
Remorse from power. And, to speak truth of Caesar,
I have not known when his affections swayed   20
More than his reason. But 'tis a common proof

22: **lowliness is young ambition's ladder:** feigned humility is the means by which the ambitious climb

24: **round:** rung

26: **base degrees:** lower rungs and those of a lower station

28: **prevent:** i.e., forestall this tyranny

29: **will bear no color for the thing he is:** will not withstand any scrutiny, considering what Caesar is like right now

30: **fashion it thus:** put it this way

31: **extremities:** extremes

33: **as his kind:** according to his nature, like others of his type

35: **closet:** private room, study

36: **flint:** stone commonly used to strike a fire

44: **exhalations:** meteors

That lowliness is young ambition's ladder,
Whereto the climber-upward turns his face;
But when he once attains the upmost round
He then unto the ladder turns his back,   25
Looks in the clouds, scorning the base degrees
By which he did ascend. So Caesar may.
Then, lest he may, prevent. And since the quarrel
Will bear no color for the thing he is,
Fashion it thus: that what he is, augmented,   30
Would run to these and these extremities.
And therefore think him as a serpent's egg
Which, hatched, would, as his kind, grow mischievous,
And kill him in the shell.

Enter LUCIUS

LUCIUS
The taper burneth in your closet, sir.   35
Searching the window for a flint, I found
This paper, thus sealed up, and I am sure,
It did not lie there when I went to bed.

Gives [BRUTUS] the letter

BRUTUS
Get you to bed again, it is not day.
Is not tomorrow, boy, the ides of March?   40

LUCIUS
I know not, sir.

BRUTUS
Look in the calendar, and bring me word.

LUCIUS
I will, sir.

Exit

BRUTUS
The exhalations, whizzing in the air,
Give so much light that I may read by them.   45

tracks 8-10

46–58:
George Coulouris as Brutus
John Bowe as Brutus

46: "*Brutus, thou sleep'st. Awake, and see thyself*": Robert Stattel as Brutus in the Shakespeare Theatre Company's 1993–94 production directed by Joe Dowling
Photo: Richard Anderson

47: **redress:** remedy
51: **piece it out:** fill in the missing pieces
59: **March is wasted fifteen days:** i.e., it is the morning of the ides of March
61: **whet:** goad, provoke
64: **motion:** impulse
65: **phantasma:** hallucination, vision
66: **genius:** governing spirit
66: **mortal instruments:** the body's organs
67: **in council:** in debate
67–68: **state of man, like to a little kingdom:** the correspondence between the human body and the body politic was commonplace in the Renaissance
70: **brother:** (actually, brother-in-law; Cassius married Brutus's sister, Junia Tertia)

Opens the letter and reads

Brutus, thou sleep'st. Awake, and see thyself.
Shall Rome, etc. Speak, strike, redress.
"Brutus, thou sleep'st; awake."
Such instigations have been often dropped
Where I have took them up.   50
"Shall Rome, etc." Thus must I piece it out:
Shall Rome stand under one man's awe? What, Rome?
My ancestors did from the streets of Rome
The Tarquin drive when he was called a king.
"Speak, strike, redress." Am I entreated   55
To speak and strike? O Rome, I make thee promise,
If the redress will follow, thou receivest
Thy full petition at the hand of Brutus.

Enter LUCIUS

LUCIUS
Sir, March is wasted fifteen days.

Knock within

BRUTUS
'Tis good. Go to the gate; somebody knocks.   60
[Exit LUCIUS]

Since Cassius first did whet me against Caesar
I have not slept.
Between the acting of a dreadful thing
And the first motion, all the interim is
Like a phantasma or a hideous dream.   65
The genius and the mortal instruments
Are then in council, and the state of man,
Like to a little kingdom, suffers then
The nature of an insurrection.

Enter LUCIUS

LUCIUS
Sir, 'tis your brother Cassius at the door,   70
Who doth desire to see you.

BRUTUS
                    Is he alone?

72: **moe:** a form of "more" (In the sixteenth century, "moe" was used to indicate a larger number and "more," a larger degree.)

75: **discover:** identify

76: **favor:** appearance

79: **most free:** move about most freely

83: **path:** pursue a path

83: **thy native semblance on:** without disguise

84: **Erebus:** the dark place in the underworld through which dead souls passed on their way to Hades

85: **prevention:** being detected, and thus being forestalled

86: **we are too bold upon your rest:** we intrude too brazenly, interrupting your sleep

Scene: Kemble (1812) heightened the drama of the conspirators revealing themselves to Brutus by having them unmuffle one at a time as Cassius introduced them. By contrast, Mankiewicz (1953) had the men lower their hoods together, losing a considerable opportunity for suspense.

LUCIUS
No, sir, there are moe with him.

BRUTUS
                    Do you know them?

LUCIUS
No, sir, their hats are plucked about their ears,
And half their faces buried in their cloaks,
That by no means I may discover them   75
By any mark of favor.

BRUTUS
                    Let 'em enter.
                                                [Exit LUCIUS]

They are the faction. O conspiracy,
Sham'st thou to show thy dangerous brow by night,
When evils are most free? O then, by day
Where wilt thou find a cavern dark enough   80
To mask thy monstrous visage? Seek none, conspiracy,
Hide it in smiles and affability;
For if thou path, thy native semblance on,
Not Erebus itself were dim enough
To hide thee from prevention.   85
         Enter the conspirators: CASSIUS, CASCA, DECIUS,
                CINNA, METELLUS, and TREBONIUS

CASSIUS
I think we are too bold upon your rest.
Good morrow, Brutus, do we trouble you?

BRUTUS
I have been up this hour, awake all night.
Know I these men that come along with you?

98: **watchful cares:** anxiety causing sleeplessness

104: **fret:** interlace

Costume rendering for Decius Brutus from the May 28, 1957, staging by the Royal Shakespeare Company at the Shakespeare Memorial Theatre directed by Glen Byam Shaw

Rare Book and Special Collections Library, University of Illinois at Urbana-Champaign

CASSIUS
    Yes, every man of them; and no man here   90
    But honors you, and every one doth wish
    You had but that opinion of yourself
    Which every noble Roman bears of you.
    This is Trebonius.

BRUTUS
                    He is welcome hither.

CASSIUS
    This, Decius Brutus.

BRUTUS
                    He is welcome too.   95

CASSIUS
    This, Casca; this, Cinna; and this, Metellus Cimber.

BRUTUS
    They are all welcome.
    What watchful cares do interpose themselves
    Betwixt your eyes and night?

CASSIUS
    Shall I entreat a word?   100
                    BRUTUS and CASSIUS whisper

DECIUS BRUTUS
    Here lies the east. Doth not the day break here?

CASCA
    No.

CINNA
    O, pardon, sir, it doth, and yon gray lines
    That fret the clouds are messengers of day.

107: **growing:** encroaching, advancing

108: **weighing:** considering

112: **all over:** all of you

114: **face:** countenance, appearance

115: **sufferance:** suffering, distress

115: **the time's abuse:** the corruption of Caesar's reign

116: **betimes:** immediately

117: **idle:** unoccupied

118: **high-sighted tyranny:** tyranny affecting even those of high rank (image is from falconry; see also note 1.1.70–71)

119: **by lottery:** by chance or according to the tyrant's whim

123: **spur:** motivate

124: **prick:** encourage

125: **than secret Romans, that have spoke the word:** than the fact that we are Romans and are sure to keep a secret

126: **palter:** equivocate

127: **honesty to honesty engaged:** exchanges of honorable promises

129: **cautelous:** cautious, crafty

130: **carrions:** a term of contempt for those no better than corpses

133: **even:** unwavering, pure

134: **insuppressive:** indomitable

CASCA

 You shall confess that you are both deceived.   105
 Here, as I point my sword, the sun arises,
 Which is a great way growing on the south,
 Weighing the youthful season of the year.
 Some two months hence up higher toward the north
 He first presents his fire, and the high east   110
 Stands, as the Capitol, directly here.

BRUTUS

 Give me your hands all over, one by one.

CASSIUS

 And let us swear our resolution.

BRUTUS

 No, not an oath. If not the face of men,
 The sufferance of our souls, the time's abuse;   115
 If these be motives weak, break off betimes,
 And every man hence to his idle bed.
 So let high-sighted tyranny range on,
 Till each man drop by lottery. But if these,
 As I am sure they do, bear fire enough   120
 To kindle cowards and to steel with valor
 The melting spirits of women, then, countrymen,
 What need we any spur but our own cause .
 To prick us to redress? What other bond
 Than secret Romans, that have spoke the word,   125
 And will not palter? And what other oath
 Than honesty to honesty engaged,
 That this shall be, or we will fall for it?
 Swear priests, and cowards, and men cautelous,
 Old feeble carrions and such suffering souls   130
 That welcome wrongs; unto bad causes swear
 Such creatures as men doubt. But do not stain
 The even virtue of our enterprise,
 Nor th' insuppressive mettle of our spirits,
 To think that or our cause or our performance   135
 Did need an oath, when every drop of blood

138: a several bastardy: individual acts that call into question one's legitimacy as a true Roman

141: "But what of Cicero? Shall we sound him?": The conspirators in the Shakespeare Theatre of New Jersey's 2005 production directed by Brian B. Crowe
Photo: Gerry Goodstein

141: sound him: discover his opinion

144–145: silver hairs . . . good opinion: i.e., his age lends us credibility

149: gravity: dignified demeanor

150: break with him: let him know of the conspiracy

154–184:
Richard Baer as Decius, Orson Welles as Cassius, George Coulouris as Brutus
John Vickery as Decius, John de Lancie as Cassius, Stacey Keach as Brutus

That every Roman bears, and nobly bears,
Is guilty of a several bastardy,
If he do break the smallest particle
Of any promise that hath passed from him.   140

CASSIUS
But what of Cicero? Shall we sound him?
I think he will stand very strong with us.

CASCA
Let us not leave him out.

CINNA
                    No, by no means.

METELLUS
O, let us have him, for his silver hairs
Will purchase us a good opinion   145
And buy men's voices to commend our deeds.
It shall be said his judgment ruled our hands;
Our youths and wildness shall no whit appear,
But all be buried in his gravity.

BRUTUS
O, name him not; let us not break with him,   150
For he will never follow anything
That other men begin.

CASSIUS
                    Then leave him out.

CASCA
Indeed he is not fit.

DECIUS BRUTUS
Shall no man else be touched but only Caesar?

154–184:
Richard Baer as Decius, Orson Welles as Cassius, George Coulouris as Brutus
John Vickery as Decius, John de Lancie as Cassius, Stacey Keach as Brutus

155: **meet:** suitable, appropriate

157: **find of:** find

158: **contriver:** schemer

158: **means:** resources

159: **improve:** make the most of

160: **annoy:** harm

164: **envy:** malice

165: (Kemble (1812) cut both this line and 189 as part of his attempt to reduce any hint of triviality or frivolity in Antony. He also removed all of 4.1, in which Antony cynically trades his nephew's life for political gain.)

169: **come by:** gain possession of

171: **gentle:** noble

175: **subtle:** cunning

177–78: **this shall make our purpose necessary and not envious:** i.e., this will show that our plan grew out of necessity, not malice

180: **purgers:** those who purify through bleeding a patient

184: **ingrafted:** firmly planted

CASSIUS

Decius, well urged. I think it is not meet   155
Mark Antony, so well beloved of Caesar,
Should outlive Caesar. We shall find of him
A shrewd contriver. And, you know, his means,
If he improve them, may well stretch so far
As to annoy us all, which to prevent,   160
Let Antony and Caesar fall together.

BRUTUS

Our course will seem too bloody, Caius Cassius,
To cut the head off and then hack the limbs,
Like wrath in death and envy afterwards,
For Antony is but a limb of Caesar.   165
Let's be sacrificers, but not butchers, Caius.
We all stand up against the spirit of Caesar,
And in the spirit of men there is no blood.
O that we then could come by Caesar's spirit
And not dismember Caesar! But, alas,   170
Caesar must bleed for it. And, gentle friends,
Let's kill him boldly, but not wrathfully;
Let's carve him as a dish fit for the gods,
Not hew him as a carcass fit for hounds.
And let our hearts, as subtle masters do,   175
Stir up their servants to an act of rage
And after seem to chide 'em. This shall make
Our purpose necessary and not envious;
Which so appearing to the common eyes,
We shall be called purgers, not murderers.   180
And for Mark Antony, think not of him,
For he can do no more than Caesar's arm
When Caesar's head is off.

CASSIUS
                    Yet I fear him,
For in the ingrafted love he bears to Caesar—

186: **all:** all the harm

187: **take thought:** suffer grief or melancholy

188: **much he should:** too much to expect from him

189: (This line, along with 165, was cut in Kemble's 1812 production)

190: **no fear in him:** no need to fear him

196: **quite from the main opinion:** different from the strongly-held belief

197: **ceremonies:** omens

198: **apparent prodigies:** visible omens

200: **augurers:** those who practiced divination according to omens and advised officials on matters of state

201: **hold:** keep

204: **unicorns may be betrayed with trees:** legend held that unicorns could be caught by causing them to charge at trees, entrapping them when their horns lodged in the tree trunks

205: **bears with glasses:** it was believed that bears could be confused by their image in a mirror

205: **holes:** large camouflaged pits

206: **toils:** nets, snares

BRUTUS

Alas, good Cassius, do not think of him.   185
If he love Caesar, all that he can do
Is to himself, take thought and die for Caesar.
And that were much he should, for he is given
To sports, to wildness, and much company.

TREBONIUS

There is no fear in him; let him not die,   190
For he will live and laugh at this hereafter.

Clock strikes

BRUTUS

Peace, count the clock.

CASSIUS

The clock hath stricken three.

TREBONIUS

'Tis time to part.

CASSIUS

But it is doubtful yet
Whether Caesar will come forth today, or no,
For he is superstitious grown of late,   195
Quite from the main opinion he held once
Of fantasy, of dreams and ceremonies.
It may be these apparent prodigies,
The unaccustomed terror of this night,
And the persuasion of his augurers   200
May hold him from the Capitol today.

DECIUS BRUTUS

Never fear that. If he be so resolved,
I can o'ersway him, for he loves to hear
That unicorns may be betrayed with trees,
And bears with glasses, elephants with holes,   205
Lions with toils and men with flatterers.
But when I tell him he hates flatterers,

210: **give his humor the true bent:** manipulate his inclinations in the proper manner

213: **uttermost:** latest

215: **bear Caesar hard:** bears a grudge against Caesar

216: **rated:** berated

218: **by:** to

220: **fashion:** shape, convince

225: **put on:** reveal

227: **untired:** unwavering

227: **formal constancy:** outward appearance of steadfastness

Stage direction: **Manet Brutus:** Brutus remains

231: **figures:** imaginings

Metellus Cimber costume rendering from the May 28, 1957, staging by the Royal Shakespeare Company at the Shakespeare Memorial Theatre directed by Glen Byam Shaw

Rare Book and Special Collections Library, University of Illinois at Urbana-Champaign

He says he does, being then most flatterèd.
Let me work,
For I can give his humor the true bent,   210
And I will bring him to the Capitol.

CASSIUS
Nay, we will all of us be there to fetch him.

BRUTUS
By the eighth hour, is that the uttermost?

CINNA
Be that the uttermost, and fail not then.

METELLUS CIMBER
Caius Ligarius doth bear Caesar hard,   215
Who rated him for speaking well of Pompey.
I wonder none of you have thought of him.

BRUTUS
Now, good Metellus, go along by him.
He loves me well, and I have given him reasons.
Send him but hither, and I'll fashion him.   220

CASSIUS
The morning comes upon 's. We'll leave you, Brutus.
And, friends, disperse yourselves, but all remember
What you have said, and show yourselves true Romans.

BRUTUS
Good gentlemen, look fresh and merrily.
Let not our looks put on our purposes,   225
But bear it as our Roman actors do,
With untired spirits and formal constancy.
And so good morrow to you every one.

                                    Exeunt. Manet BRUTUS.

Boy! Lucius! Fast asleep? It is no matter,
Enjoy the honey-heavy dew of slumber.   230
Thou hast no figures, nor no fantasies

232: **care:** anxieties

233–304:
Margaret Curtis as Portia, George Coulouris as Brutus
JoBeth Williams as Portia, Stacey Keach as Brutus

237–238: "Y'have ungently, Brutus, / Stole from my bed": Evelyn Millard as Portia and Lewis Waller as Brutus in Sir Henry Beerbohm Tree's 1898 production at Her Majesty's Theatre, London
Courtesy: Harry Rusche

237: **ungently:** disrespectfully, roughly

238: **stole:** snuck away

240: **across:** crossed, the standard Elizabethan pose indicating deep or sad thought

246: **wafture:** waving

250: **effect of humor:** moodiness

251: **his:** its

254: **condition:** state of mind

255: **know you Brutus:** recognize you as Brutus

259: **come by:** attain

Which busy care draws in the brains of men,
Therefore thou sleep'st so sound.

Enter PORTIA

PORTIA
                    Brutus, my lord.

BRUTUS
    Portia, what mean you? Wherefore rise you now?
    It is not for your health thus to commit   235
    Your weak condition to the raw cold morning.

PORTIA
    Nor for yours neither. Y'have ungently, Brutus,
    Stole from my bed; and yesternight, at supper,
    You suddenly arose and walked about,
    Musing and sighing, with your arms across,   240
    And when I asked you what the matter was,
    You stared upon me with ungentle looks.
    I urged you further, then you scratched your head,
    And too impatiently stamped with your foot.
    Yet I insisted, yet you answered not,   245
    But with an angry wafture of your hand
    Gave sign for me to leave you. So I did,
    Fearing to strengthen that impatience
    Which seemed too much enkindled, and withal
    Hoping it was but an effect of humor,   250
    Which sometime hath his hour with every man.
    It will not let you eat, nor talk, nor sleep,
    And could it work so much upon your shape
    As it hath much prevailed on your condition,
    I should not know you Brutus. Dear my lord,   255
    Make me acquainted with your cause of grief.

BRUTUS
    I am not well in health, and that is all.

PORTIA
    Brutus is wise, and, were he not in health,
    He would embrace the means to come by it.

tracks 14-16

233–304:
Margaret Curtis as Portia, George Coulouris as Brutus
JoBeth Williams as Portia, Stacey Keach as Brutus

261: **physical:** healthy

262: **unbracèd:** with doublet open or undone (see note to 1.3.48)

262: **humors:** dampness

266: **tempt:** risk, test

266: **rheumy:** causing illness

266: **unpurgèd:** impure

268: **sick offense:** harmful illness

271: **charm:** entreat

273: **incorporate:** make into a single body

274: **your half:** i.e., your wife

275: **heavy:** burdened, sad

276: **had resort to:** met with

281: **excepted:** made an exception that

283: **in sort or limitation:** (legal terms related to the tenure of land) only within limits

285: **suburbs:** outskirts (in Shakespeare's England, prostitutes plied their trade in the suburbs)

289: **ruddy drops:** blood

BRUTUS
Why, so I do. Good Portia, go to bed.   260

PORTIA
Is Brutus sick? And is it physical
To walk unbracèd and suck up the humors
Of the dank morning? What, is Brutus sick?
And will he steal out of his wholesome bed
To dare the vile contagion of the night   265
And tempt the rheumy and unpurgèd air
To add unto his sickness? No, my Brutus,
You have some sick offense within your mind,
Which, by the right and virtue of my place,
I ought to know of. And, upon my knees,   270
I charm you, by my once commended beauty,
By all your vows of love and that great vow
Which did incorporate and make us one,
That you unfold to me, yourself, your half,
Why you are heavy, and what men tonight   275
Have had resort to you, for here have been
Some six or seven who did hide their faces
Even from darkness.

BRUTUS
                        Kneel not, gentle Portia.

PORTIA
I should not need, if you were gentle Brutus.
Within the bond of marriage, tell me, Brutus,   280
Is it excepted I should know no secrets
That appertain to you? Am I yourself
But, as it were, in sort or limitation,
To keep with you at meals, comfort your bed,
And talk to you sometimes? Dwell I but in the suburbs   285
Of your good pleasure? If it be no more,
Portia is Brutus' harlot, not his wife.

BRUTUS
You are my true and honorable wife,
As dear to me as are the ruddy drops
That visit my sad heart.   290

tracks 14–16

233–304:
Margaret Curtis as Portia, George Coulouris as Brutus
JoBeth Williams as Portia, Stacey Keach as Brutus

292: **withal:** also

295: **Cato's daughter:** Marcus Porcius Cato Uticensis (95–46 BCE) was known for his strict morality and fought with Pompey against Caesar, finally committing suicide rather than being captured

299: **strong proof of my constancy:** given my resolve a difficult test

302–303: "O ye gods, / Render me worthy of this noble wife!": Robert Cuccioli as Brutus and Roxanna Hope as Portia in the Shakespeare Theatre of New Jersey's 2005 production directed by Brian B. Crowe
Photo: Gerry Goodstein

307: **construe:** explain

308: **all the charactery of:** all that is written on (i.e., the meaning of)

312: **how?:** how are you?

313: **vouchsafe:** receive graciously

PORTIA
    If this were true, then should I know this secret.
    I grant I am a woman, but withal
    A woman that Lord Brutus took to wife.
    I grant I am a woman, but withal
    A woman well-reputed, Cato's daughter.   295
    Think you I am no stronger than my sex,
    Being so fathered and so husbanded?
    Tell me your counsels, I will not disclose 'em.
    I have made strong proof of my constancy,
    Giving myself a voluntary wound   300
    Here, in the thigh. Can I bear that with patience
    And not my husband's secrets?

BRUTUS
                    O ye gods,
    Render me worthy of this noble wife!

                                                            Knock

    Hark, hark, one knocks. Portia, go in awhile,
    And by and by thy bosom shall partake   305
    The secrets of my heart.
    All my engagements I will construe to thee,
    All the charactery of my sad brows.
    Leave me with haste.

                                        Exit PORTIA
                              Enter LUCIUS and LIGARIUS
                    Lucius, who's that knocks?

LUCIUS
    He is a sick man that would speak with you.   310

BRUTUS
    Caius Ligarius, that Metellus spake of.
    Boy, stand aside.

                                        [Exit LUCIUS]
                    Caius Ligarius, how?

LIGARIUS
    Vouchsafe good morrow from a feeble tongue.

314: **brave:** noble

315: **wear a kerchief:** in Elizabethan England, a sick person would apply a poultice to his or her head and wrap it in a handkerchief (kerchief)

319: **healthful:** healthy

324: **mortified:** deadened

327: **whole:** healthy (i.e., free from tyranny)

331: **to whom:** to the house of him to whom

331: **set on your foot:** move ahead, advance

Ligarius costume rendering from the May 28, 1957, staging by the Royal Shakespeare Company at the Shakespeare Memorial Theatre directed by Glen Byam Shaw

Rare Book and Special Collections Library, University of Illinois at Urbana-Champaign

BRUTUS

O, what a time have you chose out, brave Caius,
To wear a kerchief! Would you were not sick.   315

LIGARIUS

I am not sick, if Brutus have in hand
Any exploit worthy the name of honor.

BRUTUS

Such an exploit have I in hand, Ligarius,
Had you a healthful ear to hear of it.

LIGARIUS

By all the gods that Romans bow before,   320
I here discard my sickness. Soul of Rome,
Brave son, derived from honorable loins,
Thou, like an exorcist, hast conjured up
My mortified spirit. Now bid me run,
And I will strive with things impossible,   325
Yea, get the better of them. What's to do?

BRUTUS

A piece of work that will make sick men whole.

LIGARIUS

But are not some whole that we must make sick?

BRUTUS

That must we also. What it is, my Caius,
I shall unfold to thee, as we are going   330
To whom it must be done.

LIGARIUS

                         Set on your foot,
And with a heart new-fired I follow you,
To do I know not what, but it sufficeth
That Brutus leads me on.

BRUTUS

                         Follow me, then.

                                        Thunder. Exeunt.

Location: Caesar's house

Stage direction: **nightgown:** dressing gown

5: **present:** immediate

6: **opinions of success:** assessments of the auguries

10: **forth:** go forth

tracks 17-19

13–56:
Shirley Dixon as Calphurnia, Michael Feast as Caesar
Jennie Goossens as Calphurnia, John Moffatt as Caesar, Peter Williams
as the Servant

13: **stood on ceremonies:** put faith in omens

Caesar costume rendering from the May 28, 1957, staging by the Royal Shakespeare
Company at the Shakespeare Memorial Theatre directed by Glen Byam Shaw
Rare Book and Special Collections Library, University of Illinois at Urbana-Champaign

Thunder and lightning
Enter JULIUS CAESAR in his nightgown

CAESAR
Nor heaven nor earth have been at peace tonight.
Thrice hath Calphurnia in her sleep cried out,
"Help, ho! They murder Caesar!" Who's within?

Enter a SERVANT

Servant
My lord?

CAESAR
Go bid the priests do present sacrifice,   5
And bring me their opinions of success.

Servant
I will, my lord.

Exit
Enter CALPHURNIA

CALPHURNIA
What mean you, Caesar? Think you to walk forth?
You shall not stir out of your house today.

CAESAR
Caesar shall forth. The things that threatened me   10
Ne'er looked but on my back; when they shall see
The face of Caesar, they are vanishèd.

CALPHURNIA
Caesar, I never stood on ceremonies,
Yet now they fright me. There is one within,
Besides the things that we have heard and seen,   15

tracks 17-19

13–56:
Shirley Dixon as Calphurnia, Michael Feast as Caesar
Jennie Goossens as Calphurnia, John Moffatt as Caesar, Peter Williams
as the Servant

17: **whelpèd:** given birth

18: **yawned:** opened

20: **squadron:** square formation

20: **right form:** regular formation

22: **hurtled:** clashed

25: **all use:** all that is normal

27: **whose end is purposed:** that is predestined

31: **blaze:** both proclaim and burn

35: **strange:** wondrous

39: **plucking the entrails:** (entrails of sacrificed animals were examined by augurers for omens)

Recounts most horrid sights seen by the watch.
A lioness hath whelpèd in the streets,
And graves have yawned, and yielded up their dead;
Fierce fiery warriors fought upon the clouds
In ranks and squadrons and right form of war,   20
Which drizzled blood upon the Capitol;
The noise of battle hurtled in the air,
Horses did neigh, and dying men did groan,
And ghosts did shriek and squeal about the streets.
O Caesar, these things are beyond all use,   25
And I do fear them.

CAESAR
                    What can be avoided
Whose end is purposed by the mighty gods?
Yet Caesar shall go forth, for these predictions
Are to the world in general as to Caesar.

CALPHURNIA
When beggars die, there are no comets seen,   30
The heavens themselves blaze forth the death of princes.

CAESAR
Cowards die many times before their deaths,
The valiant never taste of death but once.
Of all the wonders that I yet have heard,
It seems to me most strange that men should fear,   35
Seeing that death, a necessary end,
Will come when it will come.
                                        Enter a SERVANT
                    What say the augurers?

Servant
They would not have you to stir forth today.
Plucking the entrails of an offering forth,
They could not find a heart within the beast.   40

tracks 17-19

13–56:
Shirley Dixon as Calphurnia, Michael Feast as Caesar
Jennie Goossens as Calphurnia, John Moffatt as Caesar, Peter Williams
as the Servant

41: **in shame of:** to shame

49: **confidence:** overconfidence

55–56: "Mark Antony shall say I am not well, / And, for thy humor, I will stay at home": Jill Bennett as Calphurnia and John Gielgud as Julius Caesar in the 1970 movie directed by Stuart Burge
Courtesy: Douglas Lanier

56: **humor:** whim

59: **fetch:** accompany

60: **happy:** opportune

CAESAR

    The gods do this in shame of cowardice.

    Caesar should be a beast without a heart

    If he should stay at home today for fear.

    No, Caesar shall not. Danger knows full well

    That Caesar is more dangerous than he.   45

    We are two lions littered in one day,

    And I the elder and more terrible.

    And Caesar shall go forth.

CALPHURNIA

                Alas, my lord,

    Your wisdom is consumed in confidence.

    Do not go forth today. Call it my fear   50

    That keeps you in the house, and not your own.

    We'll send Mark Antony to the Senate House,

    And he shall say you are not well today.

    Let me, upon my knee, prevail in this.

CAESAR

    Mark Antony shall say I am not well,   55

    And, for thy humor, I will stay at home.

Enter DECIUS

    Here's Decius Brutus; he shall tell them so.

DECIUS BRUTUS

    Caesar, all hail! Good morrow, worthy Caesar.

    I come to fetch you to the Senate House.

CAESAR

    And you are come in very happy time   60

    To bear my greeting to the senators

    And tell them that I will not come today.

    Cannot is false, and that I dare not, falser.

    I will not come today. Tell them so, Decius.

CALPHURNIA

    Say he is sick.

67: **graybeards:** sometimes-contemptuous term for "old men"

75: **stays:** keeps

76: **tonight:** last night

78: **lusty:** vigorous, merry

80: **apply for:** interpret as

83: "This dream is all amiss interpreted": Jessica Ires Morris as Calphurnia, William Metzo as Julius Caesar, and Raphael Peacock as Decius Brutus in the Shakespeare Theatre of New Jersey's 2005 production directed by Brian B. Crowe
Photo: Gerry Goodstein

88: **press:** crowd around

89: **tinctures, stains, relics:** tinctures and stains allude to the practice of dipping handkerchiefs in the blood of martyrs or saints; relics refer to saintly remains

89: **cognizance:** emblem worn by noblemen of a royal house

CAESAR
               Shall Caesar send a lie?   65
  Have I in conquest stretched mine arm so far,
  To be afraid to tell graybeards the truth?
  Decius, go tell them Caesar will not come.

DECIUS BRUTUS
  Most mighty Caesar, let me know some cause,
  Lest I be laughed at when I tell them so.   70

CAESAR
  The cause is in my will. I will not come,
  That is enough to satisfy the Senate.
  But for your private satisfaction,
  Because I love you, I will let you know.
  Calphurnia here, my wife, stays me at home.   75
  She dreamt tonight she saw my statue
  Which, like a fountain with an hundred spouts,
  Did run pure blood, and many lusty Romans
  Came smiling and did bathe their hands in it.
  And these does she apply for warnings, and portents,   80
  And evils imminent, and on her knee
  Hath begged that I will stay at home today.

DECIUS BRUTUS
  This dream is all amiss interpreted;
  It was a vision fair and fortunate.
  Your statue spouting blood in many pipes,   85
  In which so many smiling Romans bathed,
  Signifies that from you great Rome shall suck
  Reviving blood, and that great men shall press
  For tinctures, stains, relics, and cognizance.
  This by Calphurnia's dream is signified.   90

CAESAR
  And this way have you well expounded it.

96–97: it were a mock apt to be rendered: it would be a sarcastic comment likely to be made

102–103: dear dear love to your proceeding: deep interest in your advancement

104: reason to my love is liable: my reason, which would keep me silent, gives way to my love

112: Caesar was ne'er so much your enemy: see note 2.1.215

113: ague: fever

Publius costume rendering from the May 28, 1957, staging by the Royal Shakespeare Company at the Shakespeare Memorial Theatre directed by Glen Byam Shaw

Rare Book and Special Collections Library, University of Illinois at Urbana-Champaign

DECIUS BRUTUS
    I have, when you have heard what I can say.
    And know it now: the Senate have concluded
    To give this day a crown to mighty Caesar.
    If you shall send them word you will not come,   95
    Their minds may change. Besides, it were a mock
    Apt to be rendered, for some one to say
    "Break up the senate till another time,
    When Caesar's wife shall meet with better dreams."
    If Caesar hide himself, shall they not whisper,   100
    "Lo, Caesar is afraid?"
    Pardon me, Caesar, for my dear dear love
    To your proceeding bids me tell you this,
    And reason to my love is liable.

CAESAR
    How foolish do your fears seem now, Calphurnia!   105
    I am ashamèd I did yield to them.
    Give me my robe, for I will go.
               Enter BRUTUS, LIGARIUS, METELLUS, CASCA,
                    TREBONIUS, CINNA and PUBLIUS
    And look where Publius is come to fetch me.

PUBLIUS
    Good morrow, Caesar.

CAESAR
                Welcome, Publius.
    What, Brutus, are you stirred so early too?   110
    Good morrow, Casca. Caius Ligarius,
    Caesar was ne'er so much your enemy
    As that same ague which hath made you lean.
    What is't o'clock?

BRUTUS
             Caesar, 'tis strucken eight.

116–117: "See, Antony, that revels long a-nights, / Is notwithstanding up": Gregory Derelian as Mark Antony and William Metzo as Julius Caesar in the Shakespeare Theatre of New Jersey's 2005 production directed by Brian B. Crowe
Photo: Gerry Goodstein

129: **That every like is not the same:** (reference to a proverb) not all those who seem to be friends ("like") are actually so

129: **earns:** years, grieves

CAESAR
  I thank you for your pains and courtesy.   115

Enter ANTONY

  See, Antony, that revels long a-nights,
  Is notwithstanding up. Good morrow, Antony.

ANTONY
  So to most noble Caesar.

CAESAR
  Bid them prepare within.
  I am to blame to be thus waited for.   120
  Now, Cinna, now, Metellus. What, Trebonius,
  I have an hour's talk in store for you.
  Remember that you call on me today.
  Be near me, that I may remember you.

TREBONIUS
  Caesar, I will. *[Aside]* And so near will I be,   125
  That your best friends shall wish I had been further.

CAESAR
  Good friends, go in, and taste some wine with me,
  And we, like friends, will straightway go together.

BRUTUS
  [Aside] That every like is not the same, O Caesar,
  The heart of Brutus earns to think upon!   130

Exeunt

Location: a street in Rome

Clement Hamelin as Artemidorus, circa 1900
Courtesy: Harry Rusche

5: **bent:** directed

5: **look about you:** be wary

6: **security:** overconfidence

7: **lover:** close friend

10: **suitor:** petitioner

12: **out of the teeth of emulation:** above envious rivalry

14: **contrive:** conspire

Act 2, Scene 3]

Enter ARTEMIDORUS, [reading a paper]

ARTEMIDORUS
  Caesar, beware of Brutus, take heed of Cassius, come not near
  Casca, have an eye to Cinna, trust not Trebonius, mark well
  Metellus Cimber, Decius Brutus loves thee not, thou hast wronged
  Caius Ligarius. There is but one mind in all these men, and it is
  bent against Caesar. If thou beest not immortal, look about you.   5
  Security gives way to conspiracy. The mighty gods defend thee!
          Thy lover,
              Artemidorus
  Here will I stand till Caesar pass along,
  And as a suitor will I give him this.   10
  My heart laments that virtue cannot live
  Out of the teeth of emulation.
  If thou read this, O Caesar, thou mayst live;
  If not, the Fates with traitors do contrive.

                           Exit

Location: outside Brutus's house

6: **constancy:** resolve, self-control

9: **keep counsel:** keep a secret

10: **yet:** still

Costume rendering for Lucius from the May 28, 1957, staging by the Royal Shakespeare Company at the Shakespeare Memorial Theatre directed by Glen Byam Shaw

Rare Book and Special Collections Library, University of Illinois at Urbana-Champaign

Act 2, Scene 4]

PORTIA

   I prithee, boy, run to the Senate House.
   Stay not to answer me, but get thee gone.
   Why dost thou stay?

LUCIUS

               To know my errand, madam.

PORTIA

   I would have had thee there and here again
   Ere I can tell thee what thou shouldst do there.   5
   O constancy, be strong upon my side,
   Set a huge mountain 'tween my heart and tongue.
   I have a man's mind, but a woman's might.
   How hard it is for women to keep counsel.
   Art thou here yet?

LUCIUS

               Madam, what should I do?   10
   Run to the Capitol, and nothing else?
   And so return to you, and nothing else?

PORTIA

   Yes, bring me word, boy, if thy lord look well,
   For he went sickly forth. And take good note
   What Caesar doth, what suitors press to him.   15
   Hark, boy, what noise is that?

LUCIUS

   I hear none, madam.

18–19: "I heard a bustling rumor, like a fray, / And the wind brings it from the Capitol": Michael Littig as Lucius and Roxanna Hope as Portia in the Shakespeare Theatre of New Jersey's 2005 production directed by Brian B. Crowe
Photo: Gerry Goodstein

18: **a bustling rumor:** noisy confusion

18: **fray:** fight

20: **sooth:** truly

26: **take my stand:** take my place

PORTIA
>Prithee, listen well;
I heard a bustling rumor, like a fray,
And the wind brings it from the Capitol.

LUCIUS
Sooth, madam, I hear nothing.   20

Enter the SOOTHSAYER

PORTIA
Come hither, fellow, which way hast thou been?

SOOTHSAYER
At mine own house, good lady.

PORTIA
What is't o'clock?

SOOTHSAYER
About the ninth hour, lady.

PORTIA
Is Caesar yet gone to the Capitol?   25

SOOTHSAYER
Madam, not yet. I go to take my stand,
To see him pass on to the Capitol.

PORTIA
Thou hast some suit to Caesar, hast thou not?

SOOTHSAYER
That I have, lady, if it will please Caesar
To be so good to Caesar as to hear me.   30
I shall beseech him to befriend himself.

PORTIA
Why, know'st thou any harm's intended towards him?

Soothsayer costume rendering from the May 28, 1957, staging by the Royal Shakespeare Company at the Shakespeare Memorial Theatre directed by Glen Byam Shaw

Rare Book and Special Collections Library, University of Illinois at Urbana-Champaign

36: **praetors:** high-ranking judges

38: **more void:** less crowded, more empty

45: **commend me:** give my regards

46: **merry:** in fine spirits

SOOTHSAYER

None that I know will be, much that I fear may chance.
Good morrow to you. Here the street is narrow.
The throng that follows Caesar at the heels,   35
Of senators, of praetors, common suitors,
Will crowd a feeble man almost to death.
I'll get me to a place more void, and there
Speak to great Caesar as he comes along.

Exit

PORTIA

I must go in. Ay me, how weak a thing   40
The heart of woman is. O Brutus,
The heavens speed thee in thine enterprise.
Sure, the boy heard me. Brutus hath a suit
That Caesar will not grant. O, I grow faint.
Run, Lucius, and commend me to my lord,   45
Say I am merry. Come to me again,
And bring me word what he doth say to thee.

Exeunt

[Julius Caesar

Act 3

Location: the Capitol in Rome

Scene: Kemble (1812) staged the scene as a discovery. A flourish sounded and the shutters were drawn back to reveal an ostentatious display of power: twelve guards stood in a semicircle upstage of the seated Caesar; directly behind him were gold and silver eagles, with priests on either side of him; the Conspirators were arranged in two lines downstage of Caesar; and three senators stood in two diagonal lines that converged on Caesar's chair. The effect of Kemble's blocking was that of a funnel, focusing the audience's gaze directly at the ruler just before the Soothsayer entered as the music ceases.

3: **schedule:** note

5: **suit:** petition

6: "O Caesar, read mine first": William Metzo as Julius Caesar and David Arsenault as Artemidorus with ensemble in the Shakespeare Theatre of New Jersey's 2005 production directed by Brian B. Crowe
Photo: Gerry Goodstein

8: **what touches us ourself shall be last served:** that which concerns me personally will be dealt with last

8: **us ourself:** Caesar is using the royal we

10: **sirrah:** a contemptuous form of "sir"

10: **give place:** make way

Act 3, Scene 1]

Flourish. Enter CAESAR, BRUTUS, CASSIUS,
CASCA, DECIUS, METELLUS, TREBONIUS,
CINNA, ANTONY, LEPIDUS, ARTEMIDORUS,
PUBLIUS, [POPILIUS], and the SOOTHSAYER

CAESAR
The ides of March are come.

SOOTHSAYER
Ay, Caesar, but not gone.

ARTEMIDORUS
Hail, Caesar. Read this schedule.

DECIUS BRUTUS
Trebonius doth desire you to o'erread,
At your best leisure, this his humble suit.   5

ARTEMIDORUS
O Caesar, read mine first, for mine's a suit
That touches Caesar nearer. Read it, great Caesar.

CAESAR
What touches us ourself shall be last served.

ARTEMIDORUS
Delay not, Caesar, read it instantly.

CAESAR
What, is the fellow mad?

PUBLIUS
                    Sirrah, give place.   10

18: **makes to:** moves towards

19: **sudden:** quick, swift

19: **prevention:** being forestalled (see note 2.1.28)

21: **turn back:** return, possibly return alive

22: **constant:** firm in your resolve

24: **Caesar doth not change:** Caesar's expression does not change

Artemidorus costume rendering from the May 28, 1957, staging by the Royal
Shakespeare Company at the Shakespeare Memorial Theatre directed
by Glen Byam Shaw

Rare Book and Special Collections Library, University of Illinois at Urbana-Champaign

CASSIUS
What, urge you your petitions in the street?
Come to the Capitol.

POPILIUS
I wish your enterprise today may thrive.

CASSIUS
What enterprise, Popilius?

POPILIUS
Fare you well.

BRUTUS
What said Popilius Lena?   15

CASSIUS
He wished today our enterprise might thrive.
I fear our purpose is discoverèd.

BRUTUS
Look how he makes to Caesar. Mark him.

CASSIUS
Casca, be sudden, for we fear prevention.
Brutus, what shall be done? If this be known,   20
Cassius or Caesar never shall turn back,
For I will slay myself.

BRUTUS
Cassius, be constant.
Popilius Lena speaks not of our purposes,
For look, he smiles, and Caesar doth not change.

CASSIUS
Trebonius knows his time, for look you, Brutus,   25
He draws Mark Antony out of the way.
[Exeunt ANTONY and TREBONIUS]

28: **presently prefer:** immediately present

29: **addressed:** ready, prepared

30: **rears:** raises

33: **puissant:** powerful

36: **couchings:** bowings, prostrations

37: **fire the blood:** incite, anger

38: **preordinance and first decree:** what has been decreed and made law

39: **law of children:** the rules that children make up in their games and amend at will

39: **be not fond:** be so foolish as

40: **rebel blood:** unruly passions

41: **quality:** nature

43: **low-crookèd curtsies and base spaniel fawning:** bows as low as possible and fawning like a dog, both obsequious gestures

46: **spurn:** kick

46: **cur:** contemptuous term for a dog

51: **repealing:** recalling from exile

DECIUS BRUTUS
   Where is Metellus Cimber? Let him go
   And presently prefer his suit to Caesar.

BRUTUS
   He is addressed. Press near and second him.

CINNA
   Casca, you are the first that rears your hand.   30

CAESAR
   Are we all ready? What is now amiss
   That Caesar and his senate must redress?

METELLUS
   Most high, most mighty, and most puissant Caesar,
   Metellus Cimber throws before thy seat
   An humble heart.

CAESAR
                        I must prevent thee, Cimber.   35
   These couchings and these lowly courtesies
   Might fire the blood of ordinary men
   And turn preordinance and first decree
   Into the law of children. Be not fond
   To think that Caesar bears such rebel blood   40
   That will be thawed from the true quality
   With that which melteth fools—I mean sweet words,
   Low-crookèd curtsies and base spaniel fawning.
   Thy brother by decree is banishèd.
   If thou dost bend and pray and fawn for him,   45
   I spurn thee like a cur out of my way.
   Know, Caesar doth not wrong, nor without cause
   Will he be satisfied.

METELLUS
   Is there no voice more worthy than my own
   To sound more sweetly in great Caesar's ear   50
   For the repealing of my banished brother?

54: **freedom of repeal:** permission to have the sentence repealed (and thus, to return)

57: **enfranchisement:** restoration of citizenship

58: **moved:** persuaded

59: **pray to move:** beg others to change their minds

60: **Northern Star:** the Pole Star, which does not change position

61: **true-fixed and resting:** unmoving and unchanging

62: **fellow:** equal

63: **unnumbered:** numerous

66–84:

Harold Gould as Caesar, Rudy Hornish as Cinna, John Vickery as Decius, Jack Coleman as Casca, Stacey Keach as Brutus
John Moffatt as Caesar, Peter Ellis as Cinna, Peter Williams as Decius, Brian Haines as Casca, Patrick Wymark as Brutus

tracks 20-22

67: **apprehensive:** possessing reason, perceptive

69: **holds on his rank:** maintains his position

70: **unshaked of motion:** unswayable, firm

74: **Olympus:** mountain home of the Greek gods

75: "Great Caesar—": Raphael Peacock as Decius Brutus and William Metzo as Julius Caesar with ensemble in the Shakespeare Theatre of New Jersey's 2005 production directed by Brian B. Crowe

Photo: Gerry Goodstein

BRUTUS
    I kiss thy hand, but not in flattery, Caesar,
    Desiring thee that Publius Cimber may
    Have an immediate freedom of repeal.

CAESAR
    What, Brutus!

CASSIUS
                Pardon, Caesar; Caesar, pardon.   55
    As low as to thy foot doth Cassius fall
    To beg enfranchisement for Publius Cimber.

CAESAR
    I could be well moved, if I were as you;
    If I could pray to move, prayers would move me.
    But I am constant as the Northern Star,   60
    Of whose true-fixed and resting quality
    There is no fellow in the firmament.
    The skies are painted with unnumbered sparks,
    They are all fire and every one doth shine,
    But there's but one in all doth hold his place.   65
    So in the world: 'tis furnished well with men,
    And men are flesh and blood, and apprehensive.
    Yet in the number I do know but one
    That unassailable holds on his rank
    Unshaked of motion. And that I am he,   70
    Let me a little show it, even in this:
    That I was constant Cimber should be banished
    And constant do remain to keep him so.

CINNA
    O Caesar—

CAESAR
                Hence! Wilt thou lift up Olympus?

DECIUS BRUTUS
    Great Caesar—

tracks 20-22

66–84:
Harold Gould as Caesar, Rudy Hornish as Cinna, John Vickery as Decius,
Jack Coleman as Casca, Stacey Keach as Brutus
John Moffatt as Caesar, Peter Ellis as Cinna, Peter Williams as Decius,
Brian Haines as Casca, Patrick Wymark as Brutus

75: **bootless:** uselessly

Scene: Kemble's directions for the assassination are full and detailed, suggesting the care and thought he put into blocking the scene. Edwin Booth, who embellished Jean-Louis Jérôme's painting *La Mort de Caesar* to orient the arrangement and movement of actors in the scene, was more willing than Kemble to create in his 1871 production a warmth of spirit and acute emotion. He mimicked the painting's side focus, in which the conspirators move to the viewer's left to attack Caesar, allowing for significant natural movement. However, the effect of the citizens' realistic panic was minimized by keeping them far upstage of the action, and they ended up serving primarily as background scenery.

77: *Et tu, Brute?*: Even thou, Brutus?
80: **common pulpits:** stages or platforms for public speeches

81: "Liberty, freedom, and enfranchisement!": The conspirators in the 1970 movie directed by Stuart Burge

Courtesy: Douglas Lanier

81: **enfranchisement:** restoration of rights
83: **ambition's debt is paid:** Caesar's ambition was repaid with the assassination (and no one else will be killed)
86: **mutiny:** 1) tumult   2) rebellion

CAESAR
            Doth not Brutus bootless kneel?   75

CASCA
    Speak, hands for me!

                                    They stab CAESAR

CAESAR
    Et tu, Brute?—Then fall, Caesar.

                                                        Dies

CINNA
    Liberty! Freedom! Tyranny is dead!
    Run hence, proclaim, cry it about the streets!

CASSIUS
    Some to the common pulpits and cry out,   80
    "Liberty, freedom, and enfranchisement!"

BRUTUS
    People and senators, be not affrighted.
    Fly not, stand still! Ambition's debt is paid.

CASCA
    Go to the pulpit, Brutus.

DECIUS BRUTUS
            And Cassius too.

BRUTUS
    Where's Publius?   85

CINNA
    Here, quite confounded with this mutiny.

METELLUS
    Stand fast together, lest some friend of Caesar's
    Should chance—

89: **standing:** making a stand

94–95: "Do so, and let no man abide this deed, / But we the doers": Robert Cuccioli as Brutus with ensemble in the Shakespeare Theatre of New Jersey's 2005 production directed by Brian B. Crowe

Photo: Gerry Goodstein

94: **abide:** 1) stay here with   2) bear responsibility for

96: **amazed:** stunned, in shock

99–100: **'tis but the time . . . stand upon:** it is only the time of death and the lengthening of life that men set store by

Scene: In keeping with the stoic, decorous nobility that Kemble sought for his characters, the actor-manager replaced Brutus's rather bloodthirsty call to stoop and bathe in Caesar's gore with the slightly more restrained "On, Romans, on; / With hands and swords besmear'd in Caesar's blood."

108: **marketplace:** the Forum

BRUTUS

    Talk not of standing. Publius, good cheer.

    There is no harm intended to your person,   90

    Nor to no Roman else. So tell them, Publius.

CASSIUS

    And leave us, Publius, lest that the people,

    Rushing on us, should do your age some mischief.

BRUTUS

    Do so, and let no man abide this deed,

    But we the doers.   95

[Exeunt all but the conspirators]

Enter TREBONIUS

CASSIUS

    Where is Antony?

TREBONIUS

         Fled to his house amazed.

    Men, wives, and children stare, cry out, and run

    As it were doomsday.

BRUTUS

         Fates, we will know your pleasures.

    That we shall die we know; 'tis but the time

    And drawing days out that men stand upon.   100

CASCA

    Why, he that cuts off twenty years of life

    Cuts off so many years of fearing death.

BRUTUS

    Grant that, and then is death a benefit.

    So are we Caesar's friends, that have abridged

    His time of fearing death. Stoop, Romans, stoop,   105

    And let us bathe our hands in Caesar's blood

    Up to the elbows, and besmear our swords.

    Then walk we forth, even to the marketplace,

    And, waving our red weapons o'er our heads,

    Let's all cry "Peace, freedom and liberty!"   110

111: **wash:** soak (their hands in Caesar's blood)

113: **accents:** languages

114: "How many times shall Caesar bleed in sport": John Gielgud as Cassius and James Mason as Brutus in the 1953 movie directed by Joseph Mankiewicz
© John Springer Collection/CORBIS

114: **in sport:** for entertainment

115: **basis:** pedestal

115: **along:** stretched out

117: **knot:** group or band

120: **grace his heels:** follow him closely (as in a procession)

122: **soft:** wait

126: **honest:** honorable

127: **royal:** noble, generous

131: **be resolved:** be convinced

CASSIUS
    Stoop, then, and wash. How many ages hence
    Shall this our lofty scene be acted over
    In states unborn and accents yet unknown?

BRUTUS
    How many times shall Caesar bleed in sport,
    That now on Pompey's basis lies along   115
    No worthier than the dust?

CASSIUS
                        So oft as that shall be,
    So often shall the knot of us be called
    The men that gave their country liberty.

DECIUS BRUTUS
    What, shall we forth?

CASSIUS
                    Ay, every man away.
    Brutus shall lead, and we will grace his heels   120
    With the most boldest and best hearts of Rome.

                                    Enter a SERVANT

BRUTUS
    Soft, who comes here? A friend of Antony's.

Servant
    Thus, Brutus, did my master bid me kneel.
    Thus did Mark Antony bid me fall down,
    And, being prostrate, thus he bade me say: 125
    Brutus is noble, wise, valiant, and honest.
    Caesar was mighty, bold, royal, and loving.
    Say I love Brutus, and I honor him.
    Say I feared Caesar, honored him and loved him.
    If Brutus will vouchsafe that Antony   130
    May safely come to him and be resolved
    How Caesar hath deserved to lie in death,
    Mark Antony shall not love Caesar dead

136: **thorough:** through

136: **untrod state:** unprecedented circumstances

140: **so:** if it

142: **presently:** immediately

143: **well to friend:** as a good friend

145–146: **still falls shrewdly to the purpose:** always end up being grievously close to the actual outcome

148: "O mighty Caesar! Dost thou lie so low?": Ralph Fiennes as Mark Antony in the 2005 production at the Barbican Theatre, London directed by Deborah Warner
© Robbie Jack/ CORBIS

152: **let blood:** refers to bloodletting but also to being killed (see note 2.1.327)

152: **rank:** swollen with an illness and thus in need of having blood let

157: **bear me hard:** bear me a grudge (see note 1.2.303)

So well as Brutus living, but will follow
The fortunes and affairs of noble Brutus   135
Thorough the hazards of this untrod state
With all true faith. So says my master Antony.

BRUTUS
Thy master is a wise and valiant Roman;
I never thought him worse.
Tell him, so please him come unto this place,   140
He shall be satisfied and, by my honor,
Depart untouched.

Servant
                    I'll fetch him presently.

                                            Exit SERVANT

BRUTUS
I know that we shall have him well to friend.

CASSIUS
I wish we may. But yet have I a mind
That fears him much, and my misgiving still   145
Falls shrewdly to the purpose.

                                            Enter ANTONY

BRUTUS
But here comes Antony. Welcome, Mark Antony.

ANTONY
O mighty Caesar! Dost thou lie so low?
Are all thy conquests, glories, triumphs, spoils,
Shrunk to this little measure? Fare thee well.   150
I know not, gentlemen, what you intend,
Who else must be let blood, who else is rank.
If I myself, there is no hour so fit
As Caesar's death hour, nor no instrument
Of half that worth as those your swords, made rich   155
With the most noble blood of all this world.
I do beseech ye, if you bear me hard,

158: **purpled:** reddened (with blood)

158: **reek and smoke:** steam

159: **live:** should I live

160: **apt:** ready

161: **so:** so much

161: **mean:** means

163: **master spirits:** i.e., most important human being

169: **pitiful:** full of pity

171: **pity pity:** pity for the general wrong done to Rome drove out pity for Caesar

173: **leaden:** i.e., blunt

177: **voice:** vote

178: **dignities:** elevated ranks, state offices

181: **deliver:** tell, explain

Now, whilst your purpled hands do reek and smoke,
Fulfil your pleasure. Live a thousand years,
I shall not find myself so apt to die. 160
No place will please me so, no mean of death,
As here by Caesar, and by you cut off,
The choice and master spirits of this age.

BRUTUS
O Antony, beg not your death of us.
Though now we must appear bloody and cruel, 165
As, by our hands and this our present act,
You see we do, yet see you but our hands
And this the bleeding business they have done.
Our hearts you see not. They are pitiful;
And pity to the general wrong of Rome— 170
As fire drives out fire, so pity pity—
Hath done this deed on Caesar. For your part,
To you our swords have leaden points, Mark Antony.
Our arms, in strength of malice, and our hearts
Of brothers' temper, do receive you in 175
With all kind love, good thoughts and reverence.

CASSIUS
Your voice shall be as strong as any man's
In the disposing of new dignities.

BRUTUS
Only be patient till we have appeased
The multitude, beside themselves with fear, 180
And then we will deliver you the cause
Why I, that did love Caesar when I struck him,
Have thus proceeded.

ANTONY
                    I doubt not of your wisdom.
Let each man render me his bloody hand.
First, Marcus Brutus, will I shake with you; 185
Next, Caius Cassius, do I take your hand;
Now, Decius Brutus, yours; now yours, Metellus;

191: **credit now stands on such slippery ground:** credibility is in a precarious position (i.e., because he was Caesar's friend)

192: **conceit:** conceive, judge

196: **dearer:** more deeply

199: **most noble:** probably refers to Caesar's spirit, but can refer ironically to the conspirators

199: **corse:** corpse

202: **close:** unite, come to an agreement

204: **bayed:** brought to bay (describing an animal cornered by hunters or predators)

204: **hart:** deer, with a pun on "heart"

206: **signed in:** bearing the signs of

206: **spoil:** a hunting term referring to the division of the quarry amongst the hounds

206: **lethe:** the Lethe is the river in Hades that induced forgetfulness; here it refers more generally to a stream or liquid of death

212: **the enemies:** even the enemies

213: **then, in a friend:** yet, from a friend

213: **modesty:** moderation

216: **pricked in number of:** counted among

217: **on:** move on

Yours, Cinna; and, my valiant Casca, yours;
Though last, not least in love, yours, good Trebonius.
Gentlemen all—alas, what shall I say?   190
My credit now stands on such slippery ground
That one of two bad ways you must conceit me,
Either a coward or a flatterer.
That I did love thee, Caesar, O, 'tis true.
If then thy spirit look upon us now,   195
Shall it not grieve thee dearer than thy death
To see thy Anthony making his peace,
Shaking the bloody fingers of thy foes?
Most noble in the presence of thy corse,
Had I as many eyes as thou hast wounds,   200
Weeping as fast as they stream forth thy blood,
It would become me better than to close
In terms of friendship with thine enemies.
Pardon me, Julius! Here wast thou bayed, brave hart,
Here didst thou fall, and here thy hunters stand,   205
Signed in thy spoil and crimsoned in thy lethe.
O world! Thou wast the forest to this hart,
And this, indeed, O world, the heart of thee.
How like a deer, strucken by many princes,
Dost thou here lie?   210

CASSIUS
  Mark Antony—

ANTONY
                    Pardon me, Caius Cassius.
  The enemies of Caesar shall say this.
  Then, in a friend, it is cold modesty.

CASSIUS
  I blame you not for praising Caesar so,
  But what compact mean you to have with us?   215
  Will you be pricked in number of our friends,
  Or shall we on and not depend on you?

218: **therefore:** i.e., it was to show you I am your friend, so

223: **or else were this:** otherwise this would be

224: **regard:** consideration

227: **suitor:** petitioner

228: **produce:** bring forward

228: **marketplace:** the Forum

230: **order:** ceremony

238: **protest:** proclaim

241: **true:** fitting, appropriate

242: **advantage:** benefit

ANTONY

    Therefore I took your hands, but was, indeed,
    Swayed from the point, by looking down on Caesar.
    Friends am I with you all and love you all,   220
    Upon this hope, that you shall give me reasons
    Why and wherein Caesar was dangerous.

BRUTUS

    Or else were this a savage spectacle.
    Our reasons are so full of good regard
    That were you, Antony, the son of Caesar,   225
    You should be satisfied.

ANTONY

                That's all I seek,
    And am moreover suitor that I may
    Produce his body to the marketplace,
    And in the pulpit, as becomes a friend,
    Speak in the order of his funeral.   230

BRUTUS

    You shall, Mark Antony.

CASSIUS

                Brutus, a word with you.
    You know not what you do. Do not consent
    That Antony speak in his funeral.
    Know you how much the people may be moved
    By that which he will utter?

BRUTUS

                By your pardon,   235
    I will myself into the pulpit first,
    And show the reason of our Caesar's death.
    What Antony shall speak, I will protest
    He speaks by leave and by permission,
    And that we are contented Caesar shall   240
    Have all true rites and lawful ceremonies.
    It shall advantage more than do us wrong.

243: **fall:** happen, come to pass

Stage direction: **Manet Antony:** Antony remains

254: "O, pardon me, thou bleeding piece of earth": Gregory Derelian as Mark Antony with William Metzo as Julius Caesar in the Shakespeare Theatre of New Jersey's 2005 production directed by Brian B. Crowe

Photo: Gerry Goodstein

254–275:
Orson Welles as Mark Antony
Adrian Lester as Mark Antony
Herbert Beerbohm Tree as Mark Antony

257: **tide of times:** course of history
258: **costly:** 1) dear, precious 2) at great cost (with dire consequences)
260: **dumb mouths:** mouths that do not speak
262: **light:** descend
264: **cumber:** encumber
265: **in use:** common
266: **objects:** sights
268: **quartered:** cut to pieces
269: **choked:** stopped
269: **custom of fell deeds:** with the commonness of terrible deeds
270: **ranging:** roaming, as a predator

CASSIUS
  I know not what may fall. I like it not.

BRUTUS
  Mark Antony, here, take you Caesar's body.
  You shall not in your funeral speech blame us,   245
  But speak all good you can devise of Caesar,
  And say you do't by our permission,
  Else shall you not have any hand at all
  About his funeral. And you shall speak
  In the same pulpit whereto I am going,   250
  After my speech is ended.

ANTONY
                    Be it so.
  I do desire no more.

BRUTUS
  Prepare the body then and follow us.

                                        Exeunt. Manet ANTONY.

ANTONY
  O, pardon me, thou bleeding piece of earth,
  That I am meek and gentle with these butchers.   255
  Thou art the ruins of the noblest man
  That ever livèd in the tide of times.
  Woe to the hand that shed this costly blood.
  Over thy wounds now do I prophesy—
  Which, like dumb mouths, do ope their ruby lips,   260
  To beg the voice and utterance of my tongue—
  A curse shall light upon the limbs of men:
  Domestic fury and fierce civil strife
  Shall cumber all the parts of Italy;
  Blood and destruction shall be so in use   265
  And dreadful objects so familiar
  That mothers shall but smile when they behold
  Their infants quartered with the hands of war,
  All pity choked with custom of fell deeds;
  And Caesar's spirit, ranging for revenge,   270

254–275:
Orson Welles as Mark Antony
Adrian Lester as Mark Antony
Herbert Beerbohm Tree as Mark Antony

271: **Ate:** Greek goddess of discord, associated with moral blindness
272: **confines:** regions
273: **cry "Havoc!":** signal slaughter without restraint
273: **let slip:** unleash

Scene: Welles (1937) blacked out the lights right here, ending scene. Welles's textual cuts worked in conjunction with the swiftness of the scene change: by removing the rest of the scene, he went straight from Antony's "let slip the dogs of war" (3.1.273) to the angry crowd crying "We will be satisfied!" (3.2.1)

282: **big:** swollen or heavy with sorrow
282: **get thee apart:** move away
283: **passion:** sorrow
286: **lies:** is staying
286: **seven leagues:** about 20 miles or 35 kilometers (a league was intended to represent the distance a person could walk in an hour, roughly 3 miles or roughly 5 kilometers)
287: **post:** ride
287: **chanced:** happened
290: **hie:** go
292: **try:** test
294: **issue:** result, outcome
295: **discourse:** describe

With Ate by his side come hot from hell,
Shall in these confines with a monarch's voice
Cry "Havoc!" and let slip the dogs of war,
That this foul deed shall smell above the earth
With carrion men, groaning for burial.   275

Enter OCTAVIUS'S SERVANT

You serve Octavius Caesar, do you not?

Servant
    I do, Mark Antony.

ANTONY
    Caesar did write for him to come to Rome.

Servant
    He did receive his letters, and is coming,
    And bid me say to you by word of mouth—   280
    O Caesar!

ANTONY
    Thy heart is big, get thee apart and weep.
    Passion, I see, is catching, for mine eyes,
    Seeing those beads of sorrow stand in thine,
    Began to water. Is thy master coming?   285

Servant
    He lies tonight within seven leagues of Rome.

ANTONY
    Post back with speed, and tell him what hath chanced.
    Here is a mourning Rome, a dangerous Rome,
    No Rome of safety for Octavius yet.
    Hie hence, and tell him so. Yet, stay awhile,   290
    Thou shalt not back till I have borne this corse
    Into the marketplace. There shall I try
    In my oration how the people take
    The cruel issue of these bloody men,
    According to the which thou shalt discourse   295
    To young Octavius of the state of things.
    Lend me your hand.

                                        Exeunt

Location: the Forum in Rome

Scene: Edwin Booth, in his 1871 production, opened this scene with maximum visual impact: the curtain opened on a spectacular vista of an imagined Imperial Rome, with a Greek temple in the foreground of the scene painting and the pulpit immediately in front of it. The bare-staged Mercury Theatre production in 1937, however, accomplished a fast, if less picturesque effect by blacking out the lights at the end of the last scene and bringing them up on Brutus, Cassius, and the mob.

1: **we will be satisfied:** we demand a satisfactory explanation
2: **audience:** a hearing
4: **part the numbers:** divide the crowd
7: **public:** made in public or related to public affairs
10: **severally:** separately

tracks 27-29

12–41:
George Coulouris as Brutus
Patrick Wymark as Brutus

12: **last:** end of the speech

13: "Romans, countrymen, and lovers, hear me for my cause": Robert Cuccioli as Brutus in the Shakespeare Theatre of New Jersey's 2005 production directed by Brian B. Crowe
Photo: Gerry Goodstein

13: **lovers:** friends
14–15: **have respect to mine honor:** bear in mind my honor
15: **censure:** judge
16: **senses:** reason

Act 3, Scene 2]

Enter BRUTUS, who goes into the pulpit,
and CASSIUS, with the PLEBEIANS

Plebeians
We will be satisfied! Let us be satisfied!

BRUTUS
Then follow me and give me audience, friends.
Cassius, go you into the other street
And part the numbers.
Those that will hear me speak, let 'em stay here.   5
Those that will follow Cassius, go with him,
And public reasons shall be rendered
Of Caesar's death.

FIRST PLEBEIAN
                    I will hear Brutus speak.

SECOND PLEBEIAN
I will hear Cassius; and compare their reasons,
When severally we hear them rendered.   10
                    [Exit CASSIUS, with some of the PLEBEIANS]

THIRD PLEBEIAN
The noble Brutus is ascended. Silence!

BRUTUS
Be patient till the last.
Romans, countrymen, and lovers, hear me for my cause, and be
silent, that you may hear. Believe me for mine honor, and have
respect to mine honor, that you may believe. Censure me in your   15
wisdom and awake your senses, that you may the better judge. If
there be any in this assembly, any dear friend of Caesar's, to him
I say that Brutus' love to Caesar was no less than his. If then that

tracks 27-29

12–41:
George Coulouris as Brutus
Patrick Wymark as Brutus

26: **bondman:** slave
27: **rude:** base, vile

29–30: "If any, speak, for him have I offended. I pause for a reply": Martin Sheen as Brutus in the Public Theater's 1987–88 production directed by Stuart Vaughan
Photo: George E. Joseph

33: **question of his death:** i.e., issues that made his death necessary
33: **enrolled:** written, recorded
34: **extenuated:** diminished
35: **enforced:** emphasized significantly
39: **lover:** friend
41: In Kemble's production, Brutus exits at this point. Kemble drew attention to the dramatic importance of Antony's speech and avoided losing any of his throng with a small piece of stage business. His additional directions in his promptbook read: "A few of the Plebeians follow Brutus [as he exits]; but return when the 1st Plebeian cries—"Stay, ho! and let us etc."

friend demand why Brutus rose against Caesar, this is my answer:
not that I loved Caesar less, but that I loved Rome more. Had you 20
rather Caesar were living and die all slaves, than that Caesar
were dead to live all free men? As Caesar loved me, I weep for
him; as he was fortunate, I rejoice at it; as he was valiant, I honor
him; but, as he was ambitious, I slew him. There is tears for his
love; joy for his fortune; honor for his valour; and death for his 25
ambition. Who is here so base that would be a bondman? If any,
speak, for him have I offended. Who is here so rude that would
not be a Roman? If any, speak, for him have I offended. Who is
here so vile that will not love his country? If any, speak, for him
have I offended. I pause for a reply. 30

All
None, Brutus, none!

BRUTUS
Then none have I offended. I have done no more to Caesar than
you shall do to Brutus. The question of his death is enrolled in the
Capitol, his glory not extenuated, wherein he was worthy, nor his
offenses enforced, for which he suffered death. 35
Enter MARK ANTONY, with CAESAR'S body.

Here comes his body, mourned by Mark Antony, who, though he
had no hand in his death, shall receive the benefit of his dying, a
place in the commonwealth, as which of you shall not? With this
I depart: that, as I slew my best lover for the good of Rome, I have
the same dagger for myself, when it shall please my country to 40
need my death.

All
Live, Brutus, live, live!

FIRST PLEBEIAN
Bring him with triumph home unto his house.

SECOND PLEBEIAN
Give him a statue with his ancestors.

45–46: "Caesar's better parts / shall be crowned in Brutus": Plebeians in the Shakespeare Theatre of New Jersey's 2005 production directed by Brian B. Crowe
Photo: Gerry Goodstein

51: **do grace:** honor, respect

51: **grace his speech:** respectfully listen to his speech

52: **tending:** relating

54: **public chair:** one of the pulpits mentioned at 3.1.80

57: **beholding:** indebted

THIRD PLEBEIAN
Let him be Caesar.

FOURTH PLEBEIAN
                          Caesar's better parts   45
Shall be crowned in Brutus.

FIRST PLEBEIAN
                          We'll bring him to his house
With shouts and clamours.

BRUTUS
                          My countrymen.

SECOND PLEBEIAN
Peace, silence! Brutus speaks.

FIRST PLEBEIAN
                          Peace, ho!

BRUTUS
Good countrymen, let me depart alone,
And, for my sake, stay here with Antony.   50
Do grace to Caesar's corpse, and grace his speech
Tending to Caesar's glories, which Mark Antony,
By our permission, is allowed to make.
I do entreat you, not a man depart,
Save I alone, till Antony have spoke.   55
                                             Exit

FIRST PLEBEIAN
Stay, ho, and let us hear Mark Antony.

THIRD PLEBEIAN
Let him go up into the public chair.
We'll hear him. Noble Antony, go up.

ANTONY
For Brutus' sake, I am beholding to you.
                          [ANTONY goes into the pulpit]

tracks 30-33

66–101:
Orson Welles as Mark Antony
Adrian Lester as Mark Antony
Simon Russell Beale as Mark Antony

67–101: In the 1953 Mankiewicz film, Marlon Brando spoke these lines in order to calm the crowd, not as a self-consciously histrionic prelude to one of Shakespeare's most famous set speeches. John Houseman records how, sixteen years earlier, George Colouris, the Mercury Theatre's Antony, "had to follow a stricken but restrained and dignified Brutus, exasperatingly scrupulous and sincere in his determination not to use the execution of the dictator for his own personal or political advantage. Antony's oration, as Colouris delivered it, was the exact opposite: it was a cynical political harangue, a skillfully organized and brilliantly delivered demagogic tour de force, a catalyst whose emotional effect on the Roman mob was deliberate and premeditated."

70: **interrèd:** buried

73: **grievous:** terrible

74: **answered it:** paid the price for it

75: **under leave:** with the permission of

FOURTH PLEBEIAN
  What does he say of Brutus?

THIRD PLEBEIAN
                  He says, for Brutus' sake,   60
  He finds himself beholding to us all.

FOURTH PLEBEIAN
  'Twere best he speak no harm of Brutus here.

FIRST PLEBEIAN
  This Caesar was a tyrant.

THIRD PLEBEIAN
                  Nay, that's certain.
  We are blest that Rome is rid of him.

SECOND PLEBEIAN
  Peace, let us hear what Antony can say.   65

ANTONY
  You gentle Romans.—

All
                  Peace, ho, let us hear him!

ANTONY
  Friends, Romans, countrymen, lend me your ears.
  I come to bury Caesar, not to praise him.
  The evil that men do lives after them,
  The good is oft interrèd with their bones.   70
  So let it be with Caesar. The noble Brutus
  Hath told you Caesar was ambitious.
  If it were so, it was a grievous fault,
  And grievously hath Caesar answered it.
  Here, under leave of Brutus and the rest—   75
  For Brutus is an honorable man;
  So are they all, all honorable men—
  Come I to speak in Caesar's funeral.

tracks 30-33

66–101:
Orson Welles as Mark Antony
Adrian Lester as Mark Antony
Simon Russell Beale as Mark Antony

82: **he:** referring to Caesar

83: **general:** the state's

84: "Did this in Caesar seem ambitious?": Martin Sheen as Brutus and Al Pacino as Mark Antony in the Public Theater's 1987–88 production directed by Stuart Vaughan
Photo: George E. Joseph

86: **sterner:** more hard-hearted

89: **Lupercal:** feast of purification (see note 1.1.65)

97: **withholds:** keeps

He was my friend, faithful and just to me,
But Brutus says he was ambitious,   80
And Brutus is an honorable man.
He hath brought many captives home to Rome
Whose ransoms did the general coffers fill.
Did this in Caesar seem ambitious?
When that the poor have cried, Caesar hath wept;   85
Ambition should be made of sterner stuff.
Yet Brutus says he was ambitious,
And Brutus is an honorable man.
You all did see that on the Lupercal
I thrice presented him a kingly crown,   90
Which he did thrice refuse. Was this ambition?
Yet Brutus says he was ambitious,
And sure he is an honorable man.
I speak not to disprove what Brutus spoke,
But here I am to speak what I do know.   95
You all did love him once, not without cause;
What cause withholds you then to mourn for him?
O judgment! Thou art fled to brutish beasts,
And men have lost their reason. Bear with me,
My heart is in the coffin there with Caesar,   100
And I must pause till it come back to me.

FIRST PLEBEIAN
    Methinks there is much reason in his sayings.

SECOND PLEBEIAN
    If thou consider rightly of the matter,
    Caesar has had great wrong.

THIRD PLEBEIAN
                    Has he, masters?
    I fear there will a worse come in his place.   105

FOURTH PLEBEIAN
    Marked ye his words? He would not take the crown;
    Therefore 'tis certain he was not ambitious.

108: **dear abide:** pay dearly for

112–113: "But yesterday the word of Caesar might / Have stood against the world":
Marlon Brando as Mark Antony in the 1953 movie directed by Joseph Mankiewicz
© Bettmann/CORBIS

114: **none so poor to do him reverence:** the lowest is too high to pay Caesar respect

123: **closet:** private room, study (see note 2.1.35)

124: **commons:** common people

127: **dip their napkins . . . blood:** reference to a traditional practice
(see note 2.2.89)

127: **napkins:** handkerchiefs

131: **issue:** descendants

FIRST PLEBEIAN
If it be found so, some will dear abide it.

SECOND PLEBEIAN
Poor soul, his eyes are red as fire with weeping.

THIRD PLEBEIAN
There's not a nobler man in Rome than Antony.   110

FOURTH PLEBEIAN
Now mark him, he begins again to speak.

ANTONY
But yesterday the word of Caesar might
Have stood against the world. Now lies he there,
And none so poor to do him reverence.
O masters! If I were disposed to stir   115
Your hearts and minds to mutiny and rage,
I should do Brutus wrong and Cassius wrong,
Who, you all know, are honorable men.
I will not do them wrong. I rather choose
To wrong the dead, to wrong myself and you,   120
Than I will wrong such honorable men.
But here's a parchment with the seal of Caesar.
I found it in his closet. 'Tis his will.
Let but the commons hear this testament—
Which, pardon me, I do not mean to read—   125
And they would go and kiss dead Caesar's wounds
And dip their napkins in his sacred blood,
Yea, beg a hair of him for memory,
And, dying, mention it within their wills,
Bequeathing it as a rich legacy   130
Unto their issue.

FOURTH PLEBEIAN
We'll hear the will. Read it, Mark Antony.

All
The will, the will, we will hear Caesar's will!

134: "Have patience, gentle friends; I must not read it": Graham Winton as Mark Antony in Theater for a New Audience's 2003 production directed by Karin Coonrod
Photo: Gerry Goodstein

135: **meet:** fitting

144: **o'ershot myself:** said too much

ANTONY

    Have patience, gentle friends; I must not read it.

    It is not meet you know how Caesar loved you.   135

    You are not wood, you are not stones, but men.

    And, being men, hearing the will of Caesar,

    It will inflame you; it will make you mad.

    'Tis good you know not that you are his heirs,

    For, if you should, O, what would come of it?   140

FOURTH PLEBEIAN

    Read the will; we'll hear it, Antony.

    You shall read us the will, Caesar's will.

ANTONY

    Will you be patient? Will you stay awhile?

    I have o'ershot myself to tell you of it.

    I fear I wrong the honorable men   145

    Whose daggers have stabbed Caesar. I do fear it.

FOURTH PLEBEIAN

    They were traitors. Honorable men!

All

    The will! The testament!

SECOND PLEBEIAN

    They were villains, murderers. The will! Read the will!

ANTONY

    You will compel me, then, to read the will?   150

    Then make a ring about the corpse of Caesar,

    And let me show you him that made the will.

    Shall I descend? And will you give me leave?

Several Plebeians

    Come down.

SECOND PLEBEIAN

               Descend.

156: **hearse:** bier

158: **far:** farther

161: **mantle:** toga or cloak

164: **that day he overcame the Nervii:** a victorious battle in 57 BCE against a Belgian tribe (from the Flanders and Hainault region) in which Caesar displayed particular bravery and at which Antony was not present

166: **rent:** tear

166: **envious:** malicious

167: **be resolved:** ascertain

171: **unkindly:** cruelly and unnaturally

172: **angel:** favorite, closest friend or, perhaps, guardian angel

174: **most unkindest:** 1) cruelest   2) most unnatural (the double superlative is for emphasis)

177: **quite:** totally

THIRD PLEBEIAN

   · You shall have leave.

        [ANTONY comes down]

FOURTH PLEBEIAN
 A ring, stand round.   155

FIRST PLEBEIAN
 Stand from the hearse, stand from the body.

SECOND CITIZEN
 Room for Antony, most noble Antony.

ANTONY
 Nay, press not so upon me; stand far off.

Several Citizens
 Stand back. Room, bear back.

ANTONY
 If you have tears, prepare to shed them now.   160
 You all do know this mantle. I remember
 The first time ever Caesar put it on.
 'Twas on a summer's evening, in his tent,
 That day he overcame the Nervii.
 Look, in this place ran Cassius' dagger through.   165
 See what a rent the envious Casca made.
 Through this the well-beloved Brutus stabbed,
 And as he plucked his cursèd steel away,
 Mark how the blood of Caesar followed it,
 As rushing out of doors, to be resolved   170
 If Brutus so unkindly knocked, or no.
 For Brutus, as you know, was Caesar's angel.
 Judge, O you gods, how dearly Caesar loved him.
 This was the most unkindest cut of all.
 For when the noble Caesar saw him stab,   175
 Ingratitude, more strong than traitors' arms,
 Quite vanquished him. Then burst his mighty heart,
 And, in his mantle muffling up his face,

181: "O, what a fall was there, my countrymen!" Charlton Heston as Mark Antony
and ensemble in the 1970 movie directed by Stuart Burge
Courtesy: Douglas Lanier

183: **flourished:** triumphed, also, brandished a sword

185: **dint:** the impression made by a blow

187: **vesture:** garments

195: **about!:** get going

Even at the base of Pompey's statue,
Which all the while ran blood, great Caesar fell.   180
O, what a fall was there, my countrymen!
Then I, and you, and all of us fell down,
Whilst bloody treason flourished over us.
O, now you weep, and I perceive you feel
The dint of pity. These are gracious drops.   185
Kind souls, what, weep you when you but behold
Our Caesar's vesture wounded? Look you here,
Here is himself, marred, as you see, with traitors.

FIRST PLEBEIAN
    O piteous spectacle!

SECOND PLEBEIAN
    O noble Caesar!   190

THIRD PLEBEIAN
    O woeful day!

FOURTH PLEBEIAN
    O traitors, villains!

FIRST PLEBEIAN
    O most bloody sight!

SECOND PLEBEIAN
    We will be revenged.

All
    Revenge! About! Seek! Burn! Fire! Kill! Slay!   195
    Let not a traitor live!

ANTONY
                    Stay, countrymen.

FIRST PLEBEIAN
    Peace there, hear the noble Antony.

202: **griefs:** grudges

209: **gave me public leave to speak:** let me speak publicly

212: **right on:** directly

217: **ruffle up:** agitate, move to anger

219: **stones of Rome to rise and mutiny:** echoes Luke 19:40, in which Christ says that if his disciples "should hold their peace, the stones would immediately cry out."

Citizen costume rendering from the May 28, 1957, staging by the Royal Shakespeare Company at the Shakespeare Memorial Theatre directed by Glen Byam Shaw

Rare Book and Special Collections Library, University of Illinois at Urbana-Champaign

SECOND PLEBEIAN
We'll hear him, we'll follow him, we'll die with him.

ANTONY
Good friends, sweet friends, let me not stir you up
To such a sudden flood of mutiny.   200
They that have done this deed are honorable.
What private griefs they have, alas, I know not,
That made them do it. They are wise and honorable,
And will, no doubt, with reasons answer you.
I come not, friends, to steal away your hearts.   205
I am no orator, as Brutus is,
But, as you know me all, a plain blunt man
That love my friend, and that they know full well
That gave me public leave to speak of him.
For I have neither wit, nor words, nor worth,   210
Action, nor utterance, nor the power of speech
To stir men's blood. I only speak right on.
I tell you that which you yourselves do know,
Show you sweet Caesar's wounds, poor poor dumb mouths,
And bid them speak for me. But were I Brutus,   215
And Brutus Antony, there were an Antony
Would ruffle up your spirits and put a tongue
In every wound of Caesar that should move
The stones of Rome to rise and mutiny.

All
We'll mutiny.

FIRST PLEBEIAN
            We'll burn the house of Brutus.   220

THIRD PLEBEIAN
Away, then, come, seek the conspirators.

ANTONY
Yet hear me, countrymen, yet hear me speak.

All
Peace, ho, hear Antony, most noble Antony!

231: **every several:** individual

231: **drachmas:** silver coins (75 drachmas is not a trivial amount)

232: The added lines in the 1937 Mercury Theatre production clearly show the extent to which Welles embellished his Roman crowd's participation and, by extension, their complicity in the subsequent unrest and Antony's rise to power. After "seventy-five drachmas," eleven actors called out the following lines before Antony could resume his speech: "Caesar!"; "For all of us?"; "Seventy-five?"; "Drachmas"; "Seventy-five"; "Seventy-five"; "Caesar's seal?"; "Seventy-five"; "To every Roman"; "For every Roman"; "Caesar."

235: **orchard:** garden

237: **common pleasures:** public grounds

242: **brands:** (firebrands) burning wood

Mark Antony costume rendering from the May 28, 1957, staging by the Royal Shakespeare Company at the Shakespeare Memorial Theatre directed by Glen Byam Shaw

Rare Book and Special Collections Library, University of Illinois at Urbana-Champaign

ANTONY
    Why, friends, you go to do you know not what.
    Wherein hath Caesar thus deserved your loves?   225
    Alas, you know not. I must tell you then.
    You have forgot the will I told you of.

All
    Most true. The will, let's stay and hear the will.

ANTONY
    Here is the will, and under Caesar's seal.
    To every Roman citizen he gives,   230
    To every several man, seventy-five drachmas.

SECOND PLEBEIAN
    Most noble Caesar! We'll revenge his death!

THIRD CITIZEN
    O royal Caesar.

ANTONY
                 Hear me with patience.

All
                    Peace, ho.

ANTONY
    Moreover, he hath left you all his walks,
    His private arbors and new-planted orchards,   235
    On this side Tiber. He hath left them you,
    And to your heirs forever, common pleasures,
    To walk abroad and recreate yourselves.
    Here was a Caesar. When comes such another?

FIRST PLEBEIAN
    Never, never.—Come, away, away.   240
    We'll burn his body in the holy place,
    And with the brands fire the traitors' houses.
    Take up the body.

244: **pluck:** tear

244–245: The admen of the MGM publicity department adapted the hysteria of the crowd in these lines to their own Hollywood sensibilities and vocabularies, publishing a mock newspaper called *The Daily Chariot* with a front-page photograph of Calhern's dead Caesar, dated 16 March 44. The picture's caption read: "Caesar Slain! Brutus, Cassius Head Plot in Stabbing of Dictator; Mobs Loot City, Many Die."

245: **forms:** benches or window frames

245: **windows:** shutters

251: **straight:** go immediately

252: **upon a wish:** as I wished

252: **merry:** favorable

255: **are rid:** have ridden

256: **belike:** likely

256: **notice:** news

257: As the action ended in Booth's production, Antony leapt six feet from the pulpit before exiting right, providing great drama for the curtain drop as supernumeraries (minor actors in crowd scenes) bore Caesar's corpse offstage.

SECOND PLEBEIAN
Go fetch fire.

THIRD PLEBEIAN
Pluck down benches.

FOURTH PLEBEIAN
Pluck down forms, windows, anything.   245
Exeunt PLEBEIANS [with CAESAR'S body].

ANTONY
Now let it work. Mischief, thou art afoot;
Take thou what course thou wilt.

Enter SERVANT

How now, fellow!

Servant
Sir, Octavius is already come to Rome.

ANTONY
Where is he?

Servant
He and Lepidus are at Caesar's house.   250

ANTONY
And thither will I straight to visit him.
He comes upon a wish. Fortune is merry,
And in this mood will give us anything.

Servant
I heard him say, Brutus and Cassius
Are rid like madmen through the gates of Rome.   255

ANTONY
Belike they had some notice of the people,
How I had moved them. Bring me to Octavius.

Exeunt

Location: a street in Rome

Stage direction: **Cinna**: Gaius Helvius Cinna, a Roman poet admired by Catullus

1–34:
Richard Baer as Cinna the Poet
Arthur Hankey as Cinna the Poet and Lee Arenberg, Josh Fradon,
and Marnie Mosiman as Plebeians

1: **tonight:** last night

2: **unluckily charge my fantasy:** burden my imagination with ill omens

3: **of:** out of

Scene: This scene, which Welles brought back to the stage after years of being cut, was one of the highlights of the Mercury Theatre's *Caesar*. At this point, Cinna heard footsteps offstage, echoes of the mob's footsteps that (according to the script's additional direction) built "an increasing tempo and crescendo" as the angry citizens exited the previous scene.

12: **you were best:** it would be best for you

Act 3, Scene 3]

Enter CINNA THE POET and after him, the PLEBEIANS

CINNA THE POET
  I dreamt tonight that I did feast with Caesar,
  And things unluckily charge my fantasy.
  I have no will to wander forth of doors,
  Yet something leads me forth.

FIRST PLEBEIAN
  What is your name?   5

SECOND PLEBEIAN
  Whither are you going?

THIRD PLEBEIAN
  Where do you dwell?

FOURTH PLEBEIAN
  Are you a married man or a bachelor?

SECOND PLEBEIAN
  Answer every man directly.

FIRST PLEBEIAN
  Ay, and briefly.   10

FOURTH PLEBEIAN
  Ay, and wisely.

THIRD PLEBEIAN
  Ay, and truly, you were best.

tracks 34-36

1–34:
Richard Baer as Cinna the Poet
Arthur Hankey as Cinna the Poet and Lee Arenberg, Josh Fradon,
and Marnie Mosiman as Plebeians

16–17: **bear me a bang:** sustain a beating from me

17: **proceed directly:** answer straightforwardly, without evasion

18: **directly:** 1) straightforwardly   2) immediately   3) without detour

22: **for your dwelling:** i.e., where do you dwell?

25: Welles transposed Cinna's "I am Cinna the poet" from 27 here, and inserted a series of half lines from a moment of civil unrest in Shakespeare's final tragedy, *Coriolanus*: "What shouts are these?"; "The other side o'th'city is risen"; "Why stay we here?"; "To the Capitol!"; "One word, good citizens"; "No more talking on't."

CINNA THE POET
   What is my name? Whither am I going? Where do I dwell? Am I
   a married man or a bachelor? Then, to answer every man directly
   and briefly, wisely and truly. Wisely I say I am a bachelor.   15

SECOND PLEBEIAN
   That's as much as to say, they are fools that marry. You'll bear me
   a bang for that, I fear. Proceed directly.

CINNA THE POET
   Directly I am going to Caesar's funeral.

FIRST PLEBEIAN
   As a friend or an enemy?

CINNA THE POET
   As a friend.   20

SECOND PLEBEIAN
   That matter is answered directly.

FOURTH PLEBEIAN
   For your dwelling, briefly.

CINNA THE POET
   Briefly, I dwell by the Capitol.

THIRD PLEBEIAN
   Your name, sir, truly.

CINNA THE POET
   Truly, my name is Cinna.   25

FIRST PLEBEIAN
   Tear him to pieces, he's a conspirator.

CINNA THE POET
   I am Cinna the poet, I am Cinna the poet.

1–34:
Richard Baer as Cinna the Poet
Arthur Hankey as Cinna the Poet and Lee Arenberg, Josh Fradon,
and Marnie Mosiman as Plebeians

28: "Tear him for his bad verses, tear him for his bad verses": Chris Harris as Cinna
the poet torn apart by the angry mob (Robert Oates, Arthur Whybrow, and Sidney
Livingstone) in the Royal Shakespeare Company's 1972 production directed by
Trevor Nunn

© Royal Shakespeare Company

31: **turn him going:** dispatch him

FOURTH PLEBEIAN
Tear him for his bad verses, tear him for his bad verses.

CINNA THE POET
I am not Cinna the conspirator.

FOURTH PLEBEIAN
It is no matter, his name's Cinna. Pluck but his name out of his   30
heart, and turn him going.

THIRD PLEBEIAN
Tear him, tear him! Come, brands, ho! Firebrands! To Brutus', to
Cassius', burn all! Some to Decius' house, and some to Casca's,
some to Ligarius'! Away, go!

Exeunt

[Julius Caesar

Act 4

Location: Antony's house

Scene: Kemble (1812) cut this scene, in which Antony cynically trades his nephew's life for political gain, as part of his attempt to reduce any hint of triviality or frivolity in Antony. He cut lines 2.1.165 and 2.1.189 for the same reason.

Mankiewicz's film kept this scene, and the director used it to emphasize Antony's political opportunism. The film gradually deflates the excitement of Antony's impassioned rhetoric and the mob's destructiveness by showing us Antony smiling slightly at his effect on the crowd (3.2.240) and by showing the mayhem's rather inglorious dénouement: a pile of garbage burning in the middle of the forum as a few citizens mill about aimlessly. The screen then fades to Antony, Lepidus, and Octavius discussing their plans in Caesar's palace: Brando's Antony dooms his nephew to death, intoning with utter apathy, "He shall not live. Look, with a spot I damn him" (6). Shortly afterwards, Brando gives his Antony a wholly cynical spin, speaking with contempt of Lepidus as though he were a horse only to follow Antony's command (29–40). The director completes the contrast between this cynicism and Antony's previous rhetoric with some silent extratextual stage business. The camera follows Brando, alone in Caesar's chamber, as his Antony walks over to Caesar's bust and turns the statue towards him, smiling meditatively. As Antony picks up a map and sits in Caesar's chair, the dead leader's musical theme sounds to signal a continuation of ruthless rule. If Brando had to stretch himself for his scenes of high-blown Shakespearean rhetoric, this short, wordless episode that drew on body language and subtle facial expression to project deep inner psychological processes was perfectly suited to the performer's background in Method acting.

1: **pricked:** marked on a list (with a prick mark)

2: **brother:** Lucius Aemilius Paulus, Lepidius's elder brother who supported Brutus but escaped assassination

4: **Publius:** likely a mistake, for Antony did not have a nephew named Publius

6: **spot:** mark

6: **damn:** condemn

9: **cut off some charge in legacies:** reduce the cost of Caesar's bequests

Act 4, Scene 1]

Enter ANTONY, OCTAVIUS, and LEPIDUS

ANTONY
These many, then, shall die; their names are pricked.

OCTAVIUS
Your brother too must die; consent you, Lepidus?

LEPIDUS
I do consent.

OCTAVIUS
                Prick him down, Antony.

LEPIDUS
Upon condition Publius shall not live,
Who is your sister's son, Mark Antony.   5

ANTONY
He shall not live. Look, with a spot I damn him.
But, Lepidus, go you to Caesar's house.
Fetch the will hither, and we shall determine
How to cut off some charge in legacies.

LEPIDUS
What, shall I find you here?   10

OCTAVIUS
Or here, or at the Capitol.

Exit LEPIDUS

12: **slight unmeritable:** insignificant and without merit

14: **threefold world:** the Roman world was divided into Africa and Asia, and Europe

14: **divided:** the Roman world was divided among the triumvirate as follows: Antony governed Gaul; Lepidus governed Spain; and Octavius governed Africa, Sardinia, and Sicily.

16: **voice:** vote

17: **black sentence:** death sentence

17: **proscription:** a statute implemented by the triumvirate to declare their enemies outlaws and to seize their property

20: **divers slanderous loads:** different sorts of accusations put upon us

22: **business:** burden

26: **empty:** unburdened

27: **commons:** public lands or pastures

30: **appoint:** assign, grant

30: **store of provender:** supply of fodder

32: **wind:** turn

34: **taste:** measure

37: **arts, and imitations:** things that are artificial, faddish behavior or objects

38: **staled:** worn out or made common

39: **begin his fashion:** is for him the height of fashion

ANTONY
  This is a slight unmeritable man,
  Meet to be sent on errands. Is it fit,
  The threefold world divided, he should stand
  One of the three to share it?

OCTAVIUS
                    So you thought him   15
  And took his voice who should be pricked to die
  In our black sentence and proscription.

ANTONY
  Octavius, I have seen more days than you,
  And though we lay these honors on this man,
  To ease ourselves of divers slanderous loads,   20
  He shall but bear them as the ass bears gold,
  To groan and sweat under the business,
  Either led or driven, as we point the way;
  And having brought our treasure where we will,
  Then take we down his load, and turn him off,   25
  Like to the empty ass, to shake his ears,
  And graze in commons.

OCTAVIUS
                    You may do your will,
  But he's a tried and valiant soldier.

ANTONY
  So is my horse, Octavius, and for that
  I do appoint him store of provender.   30
  It is a creature that I teach to fight,
  To wind, to stop, to run directly on,
  His corporal motion governed by my spirit.
  And, in some taste, is Lepidus but so.
  He must be taught and trained and bid go forth;   35
  A barren-spirited fellow, one that feeds
  On objects, arts, and imitations,
  Which, out of use and staled by other men,
  Begin his fashion. Do not talk of him,

40: **property:** mere possession; also refers to its theatrical sense of "prop"

41: **listen:** hear

42: **levying powers:** raising armies

42: **straight make head:** immediately raise our army

44: **made:** confirmed and gathered

44: **stretched:** pushed to their limits

45: **presently:** immediately

47: **open perils surest answerèd:** visible threats safely managed

48–49: **at the stake, and bayed about:** the imagery is from bear-baiting, in which the bear was tied to a stake and a pack of dogs surrounded it, holding it at bay

Jeffrey Wright as Mark Antony, pricking the names of those who are a danger to their rule, in the Public Theater's 2000 production directed by Barry Edelstein
Photo: Michal Daniel

But as a property. And now, Octavius,   40
Listen great things. Brutus and Cassius
Are levying powers; we must straight make head.
Therefore let our alliance be combined,
Our best friends made, our means stretched,
And let us presently go sit in council,   45
How covert matters may be best disclosed
And open perils surest answerèd.

OCTAVIUS
Let us do so, for we are at the stake,
And bayed about with many enemies,
And some that smile have in their hearts, I fear,   50
Millions of mischiefs.

Exeunt

Location: the military encampment near Sardis, at Brutus's tent

Scene: By cutting the Proscription scene (4.1), in which Antony, Octavius, and Lepidus plan to kill their enemies, Welles cleverly made a direct transition from the suggested violence of the Cinna the Poet scene to the promise of violence in the moments preceding Brutus's encounter with Cassius. After Cinna the Poet was rushed away by the citizens, his frenzied offstage cry was heard, the lights then dimmed, and, to the accompaniment of loud drums and organ, a column of helmeted soldiers emerged out of the semi-darkness (just as the murderous crowd had in the previous scene) and filed across the stage.

1: **stand ho:** halt

6: **he greets me well:** he sends a good man as a messenger

7: **in his own change:** whether he has changed

7: **ill:** bad, wrong

8: **worthy:** significant, good

10: **be satisfied:** be given an explanation

12: **full of regard:** worthy of respect

14: **resolved:** informed

Act 4, Scene 2]

Drum
Enter BRUTUS, LUCILIUS, [LUCIUS], and the army
TITINIUS and PINDARUS meet them

BRUTUS
Stand ho!

LUCILIUS
Give the word ho, and stand!

BRUTUS
What now, Lucilius, is Cassius near?

LUCILIUS
He is at hand, and Pindarus is come
To do you salutation from his master.   5

BRUTUS
He greets me well. Your master, Pindarus,
In his own change, or by ill officers,
Hath given me some worthy cause to wish
Things done, undone; but if he be at hand
I shall be satisfied.

PINDARUS
                           I do not doubt   10
But that my noble master will appear
Such as he is, full of regard and honor.

BRUTUS
He is not doubted. A word, Lucilius;
How he received you, let me be resolved.

16: **familiar instances:** signs of friendship

17: **conference:** conversation

19: **ever:** always

21: **an enforced ceremony:** forced behavior

22: **tricks:** falsehoods

23: **hollow:** insincere

23: **hot at hand:** fiery at the start

26: **fall:** let fall

26: **crests:** the ridges along a horse's neck

26: **jades:** broken down (and therefore, worthless) horses

27: **sink in the trial:** fail the test

28: **Sardis:** the capital of Lydia in Asia Minor

Scene: John Houseman recalls of the tent scene in the 1953 film: "Brutus's stoic honesty and his belated, despairing realization that violence only breeds violence was admirably conveyed by Mason . . ." Houseman then discusses the tradition of treating Brutus as the play's natural central character, but points to the danger in casting a good actor as Brutus against a Cassius played by one of the twentieth century's *greatest* actors: "Gielgud surpassed himself. His Cassius was so human and so affecting in his submission to the wrongheaded but morally superior Brutus that, at his death, he had almost become the hero of our tragedy."

29: **horse in general:** the majority of the cavalry

31: **gently:** carefully, without hostility

33: **speak the word along:** i.e., pass on the word

LUCILIUS
  With courtesy and with respect enough,   15
  But not with such familiar instances,
  Nor with such free and friendly conference,
  As he hath used of old.

BRUTUS
                Thou hast described
  A hot friend cooling. Ever note, Lucilius,
  When love begins to sicken and decay   20
  It useth an enforced ceremony.
  There are no tricks in plain and simple faith,
  But hollow men, like horses hot at hand,
  Make gallant show and promise of their mettle.

                      Low march within
  But when they should endure the bloody spur,   25
  They fall their crests, and, like deceitful jades,
  Sink in the trial. Comes his army on?

LUCILIUS
  They mean this night in Sardis to be quartered.
  The greater part, the horse in general,
  Are come with Cassius.
               Enter CASSIUS and his powers

BRUTUS
             Hark, he is arrived.   30
  March gently on to meet him.

CASSIUS
  Stand ho!

BRUTUS
  Stand ho! Speak the word along.

FIRST SOLDIER
  Stand!

SECOND SOLDIER
  Stand!   35

40: **sober form:** outward seriousness

41: **content:** calm

42: **griefs:** grievances

46: **enlarge:** fully express

Tent scene. Set rendering from the May 28, 1957, staging by the Royal Shakespeare Company at the Shakespeare Memorial Theatre directed by Glen Byam Shaw
Rare Book and Special Collections Library, University of Illinois at Urbana-Champaign

54: **noted:** publicly disgraced

56: **praying:** pleading

57: **slighted off:** casually dismissed

THIRD SOLDIER
Stand!

CASSIUS
Most noble brother, you have done me wrong.

BRUTUS
Judge me, you gods; wrong I mine enemies?
And, if not so, how should I wrong a brother?

CASSIUS
Brutus, this sober form of yours hides wrongs,   40
And when you do them—

BRUTUS
                    Cassius, be content.
Speak your griefs softly. I do know you well.
Before the eyes of both our armies here,
Which should perceive nothing but love from us,
Let us not wrangle. Bid them move away.   45
Then in my tent, Cassius, enlarge your griefs,
And I will give you audience.

CASSIUS
                    Pindarus,
Bid our commanders lead their charges off
A little from this ground.

BRUTUS
Lucius, do you the like, and let no man   50
Come to our tent till we have done our conference.
Let Lucilius and Titinius guard our door.
                    Exeunt. Manet BRUTUS and CASSIUS.

CASSIUS
That you have wronged me doth appear in this.
You have condemned and noted Lucius Pella
For taking bribes here of the Sardians,   55
Wherein my letters, praying on his side,
Because I knew the man, was slighted off.

59: **meet:** appropriate

60: **nice:** petty

60: **his comment:** its criticism

62: **to have:** of having

62: **itching palm:** greedy

63: **mart:** market

64: An extra direction in Kemble's promptbook indicates that Cassius "Half-draws his sword" on this line, harkening back to the early seventeenth-century tradition of the two arguing men threatening to draw their swords that Leonard Digges mentions in his 1640 dedicatory poem (see page two).

67: **honors:** lends credibility to

68: **chastisement doth therefore hide his head:** i.e., people become reluctant to criticize

72–73: **what villain ... for justice:** who was so villainous that he stabbed Caesar for some motive other than justice?

75: **but:** only

75: **for supporting robbers:** (added reason for Caesar's assassination)

77: **mighty space of our large honors:** our exceedingly honorable reputations

78: **trash:** i.e., money

79: **bay:** howl at

BRUTUS
  You wronged yourself to write in such a case.

CASSIUS
  In such a time as this it is not meet
  That every nice offense should bear his comment.   60

BRUTUS
  Let me tell you, Cassius, you yourself
  Are much condemned to have an itching palm,
  To sell and mart your offices for gold
  To undeservers.

CASSIUS
                      I, an itching palm?
  You know that you are Brutus that speak this,   65
  Or, by the gods, this speech were else your last.

BRUTUS
  The name of Cassius honors this corruption,
  And chastisement doth therefore hide his head.

CASSIUS
  Chastisement?

BRUTUS
  Remember March, the ides of March remember.   70
  Did not great Julius bleed for justice' sake?
  What villain touched his body, that did stab,
  And not for justice? What, shall one of us
  That struck the foremost man of all this world,
  But for supporting robbers, shall we now   75
  Contaminate our fingers with base bribes
  And sell the mighty space of our large honors
  For so much trash as may be graspèd thus?
  I had rather be a dog and bay the moon
  Than such a Roman.

82: **hedge me in:** limit my authority

84: **make conditions:** manage things

88: **urge:** push, provoke

89: **health:** well-being

89: **tempt:** test

90: **slight:** insignificant

92: **choler:** anger, temper

93: "Must I give way and room to your rash choler?": Robert Cuccioli as Brutus and Richard Topol as Cassius in the Shakespeare Theatre of New Jersey's 2005 production directed by Brian B. Crowe
Photo: Gerry Goodstein

97: **bondmen:** slaves

97: **budge:** flinch

98: **observe:** pay heed to, respect

98: **crouch:** bow down

CASSIUS
>Brutus, bait not me.   80
I'll not endure it. You forget yourself
To hedge me in. I am a soldier, I,
Older in practice, abler than yourself
To make conditions.

BRUTUS
Go to, you are not, Cassius.   85

CASSIUS
I am.

BRUTUS
I say you are not.

CASSIUS
Urge me no more, I shall forget myself.
Have mind upon your health, tempt me no further.

BRUTUS
Away, slight man!   90

CASSIUS
Is't possible?

BRUTUS
>Hear me, for I will speak.
Must I give way and room to your rash choler?
Shall I be frighted when a madman stares?

CASSIUS
O ye gods, ye gods, must I endure all this?

BRUTUS
All this? Ay, more. Fret till your proud heart break.   95
Go show your slaves how choleric you are,
And make your bondmen tremble. Must I budge?
Must I observe you? Must I stand and crouch

99: **testy humor:** irritability

100: **digest the venom of your spleen:** i.e., swallow your poisonous anger

101: **though it do split you:** (the spleen was thought to be the source of violent emotion)

103: **waspish:** irritable, petulant

105: **vaunting:** boasting

107: **of:** from

111: **moved:** angered, upset

Brutus costume rendering from the May 28, 1957, staging by the Royal Shakespeare Company at the Shakespeare Memorial Theatre directed by Glen Byam Shaw
Rare Book and Special Collections Library, University of Illinois at Urbana-Champaign

Under your testy humor? By the gods,
You shall digest the venom of your spleen,   100
Though it do split you. For, from this day forth,
I'll use you for my mirth, yea, for my laughter,
When you are waspish.

CASSIUS
                    Is it come to this?

BRUTUS
You say you are a better soldier.
Let it appear so; make your vaunting true,   105
And it shall please me well. For mine own part,
I shall be glad to learn of noble men.

CASSIUS
You wrong me every way, you wrong me, Brutus.
I said, an elder soldier, not a better.
Did I say "better?"

BRUTUS
                    If you did, I care not.   110

CASSIUS
When Caesar lived, he durst not thus have moved me.

BRUTUS
Peace, peace, you durst not so have tempted him.

CASSIUS
I durst not?

BRUTUS
No.

CASSIUS
What? Durst not tempt him?

BRUTUS
                    For your life you durst not.   115

116: **presume too much upon:** count too much on
118: **that:** that which
120: **honesty:** integrity
122: **respect not:** pay no heed to
124: **vile:** base, underhanded
126: **drop:** spill
127: **trash:** i.e., money
128: **indirection:** crooked method
133: **lock:** deny
133: **rascal counters:** i.e., trivial sums (counters = contemptuous term for money)

134–135: "Be ready, gods, with all your thunderbolts, / Dash him to pieces!": Robert Stattel as Brutus and Philip Goodwin as Cassius in the Shakespeare Theatre Company's 1993–94 production directed by Joe Dowling
Photo: Richard Anderson

137–170:
Orson Welles as Cassius, George Coulouris as Brutus
John de Lancie as Cassius, Stacey Keach as Brutus

tracks 37-39

137: **rived:** split, broken
138: **infirmities:** weaknesses, shortcomings
140: **practice:** impose

CASSIUS
>Do not presume too much upon my love.
>I may do that I shall be sorry for.

BRUTUS
>You have done that you should be sorry for.
>There is no terror, Cassius, in your threats,
>For I am armed so strong in honesty   120
>That they pass by me as the idle wind,
>Which I respect not. I did send to you
>For certain sums of gold, which you denied me,
>For I can raise no money by vile means.
>By heaven, I had rather coin my heart   125
>And drop my blood for drachmas than to wring
>From the hard hands of peasants their vile trash
>By any indirection. I did send
>To you for gold to pay my legions,
>Which you denied me. Was that done like Cassius?   130
>Should I have answered Caius Cassius so?
>When Marcus Brutus grows so covetous
>To lock such rascal counters from his friends,
>Be ready, gods, with all your thunderbolts,
>Dash him to pieces!

CASSIUS
>   I denied you not.   135

BRUTUS
>You did.

CASSIUS
>   I did not. He was but a fool that brought
>My answer back. Brutus hath rived my heart.
>A friend should bear his friend's infirmities,
>But Brutus makes mine greater than they are.

BRUTUS
>I do not, till you practice them on me.   140

tracks 37-39

137–170:
Orson Welles as Cassius, George Coulouris as Brutus
John de Lancie as Cassius, Stacey Keach as Brutus

148: **braved:** defied
149: **checked:** rebuked
150: **conned by rote:** memorized
151: **cast into my teeth:** i.e., throw in my face

153: "And here my naked breast": Richard Topol as Cassius and Robert Cuccioli as Brutus in the Shakespeare Theatre of New Jersey's 2005 production directed by Brian B. Crowe

Photo: Gerry Goodstein

154: **dearer:** more full of treasure
154: **Pluto:** Roman name of the god of the underworld. He was often confused with Plutus, god of Riches.
160: **it shall have scope:** your anger will be allowed full expression
161: **dishonor shall be humor:** insults will be taken as the result of a bad mood or temper
163: **carries anger as the flint bears fire:** retains an angry mood as well as a flint sustains a flame
164: **much enforcèd:** subjected to great force
165: **straight:** immediately

CASSIUS
    You love me not.

BRUTUS
                    I do not like your faults.

CASSIUS
    A friendly eye could never see such faults.

BRUTUS
    A flatterer's would not, though they do appear
    As huge as high Olympus.

CASSIUS
    Come, Antony, and young Octavius, come,   145
    Revenge yourselves alone on Cassius,
    For Cassius is aweary of the world;
    Hated by one he loves; braved by his brother;
    Checked like a bondman; all his faults observed,
    Set in a notebook, learned, and conned by rote,   150
    To cast into my teeth. O, I could weep
    My spirit from mine eyes! There is my dagger,
    And here my naked breast; within, a heart
    Dearer than Pluto's mine, richer than gold.
    If that thou be'st a Roman, take it forth.   155
    I, that denied thee gold, will give my heart.
    Strike, as thou didst at Caesar. For I know
    When thou didst hate him worst, thou lovedst him better
    Than ever thou lovedst Cassius.

BRUTUS
                    Sheathe your dagger.
    Be angry when you will, it shall have scope;   160
    Do what you will, dishonor shall be humor.
    O Cassius, you are yoked with a lamb
    That carries anger as the flint bears fire;
    Who, much enforcèd, shows a hasty spark
    And straight is cold again.

137–170:
Orson Welles as Cassius, George Coulouris as Brutus
John de Lancie as Cassius, Stacey Keach as Brutus

167: **blood ill-tempered:** unbalanced disposition

172: **rash humor:** quick temper

175: **leave you so:** let it pass

Titinius costume rendering from the May 28, 1957, staging by the Royal Shakespeare
Company at the Shakespeare Memorial Theatre directed by Glen Byam Shaw

Rare Book and Special Collections Library, University of Illinois at Urbana-Champaign

CASSIUS

               Hath Cassius lived   165
To be but mirth and laughter to his Brutus,
When grief and blood ill-tempered vexeth him?

BRUTUS

   When I spoke that, I was ill-tempered too.

CASSIUS

   Do you confess so much? Give me your hand.

BRUTUS

   And my heart too.

CASSIUS

                O Brutus!

BRUTUS

                    What's the matter?   170

CASSIUS

   Have not you love enough to bear with me,
When that rash humor which my mother gave me
Makes me forgetful?

BRUTUS

               Yes, Cassius, and from henceforth,
When you are over-earnest with your Brutus,
He'll think your mother chides, and leave you so.   175
             Enter a POET, [LUCILIUS, and TITINIUS]

Poet

   Let me go in to see the generals.
There is some grudge between 'em; 'tis not meet
They be alone.

LUCILIUS

               You shall not come to them.

179: **stay:** stop

184: **cynic:** rude man (in Shakespeare's primary source, Plutarch's *The Lives of Noble Grecians and Romans*, this poet is a Cynic philosopher)

185: **sirrah:** contemptuous form of "sir"

185: **saucy:** insolent, perhaps even insubordinate

187: **I'll know . . . his time:** I will countenance his insolence when he learns there is a right time for it

188: **jigging:** inconsequential, but it also refers to the meter of his verse and the dance performed along with the rhyming verses

Poet
Nothing but death shall stay me.

CASSIUS
How now, what's the matter?   180

Poet
For shame, you generals, what do you mean?
Love and be friends, as two such men should be,
For I have seen more years, I'm sure, than ye.

CASSIUS
Ha, ha! How vilely doth this cynic rhyme!

BRUTUS
Get you hence, sirrah; saucy fellow, hence!   185

CASSIUS
Bear with him, Brutus, 'tis his fashion.

BRUTUS
I'll know his humor when he knows his time.
What should the wars do with these jigging fools?
Companion, hence.

CASSIUS
                    Away, away, be gone.

                                               Exit POET

BRUTUS
Lucilius and Titinius, bid the commanders   190
Prepare to lodge their companies tonight.

CASSIUS
And come yourselves, and bring Messala with you
Immediately to us.

                        [Exeunt LUCILIUS and TITINIUS]

BRUTUS
Lucius, a bowl of wine!

Cassius costume rendering from the May 28, 1957, staging by the Royal Shakespeare Company at the Shakespeare Memorial Theatre directed by Glen Byam Shaw

Rare Book and Special Collections Library, University of Illinois at Urbana-Champaign

197–198: of your philosophy . . . accidental evils: your philosophy is useless if you let chance misfortunes upset you (the philosophy to which he refers is ostensibly Stoicism)

199: Though Booth (1871) was apparently stern and authoritative throughout the quarrel with Cassius, he broke down and cried on these lines. Such emotion represents a departure from the tradition of Kemble's stoic, epic heroism. Though Booth was building on Kemble's tradition, he was more adept at subtle emotion, a fact reflected in his great success in roles like Hamlet.

202: killing: being killed

203: touching: grievous

204: impatient of: unable to bear

208: swallowed fire: Plutarch records that she "took burning coals and cast them into her mouth, and kept her mouth so close that she choked herself" (173)

CASSIUS
   I did not think you could have been so angry.   195

BRUTUS
   O Cassius, I am sick of many griefs.

CASSIUS
   Of your philosophy you make no use
   If you give place to accidental evils.

BRUTUS
   No man bears sorrow better. Portia is dead.

CASSIUS
   Ha? Portia?   200

BRUTUS
   She is dead.

CASSIUS
   How 'scaped I killing when I crossed you so?
   O insupportable and touching loss!
   Upon what sickness?

BRUTUS
                        Impatient of my absence,
   And grief that young Octavius with Mark Antony   205
   Have made themselves so strong—for with her death
   That tidings came—with this she fell distract,
   And, her attendants absent, swallowed fire.

CASSIUS
   And died so?

BRUTUS
                        Even so.

CASSIUS
                        O ye immortal gods!
                        Enter Boy [LUCIUS] with wine and taper

217: **call in question:** discuss

222: **bending:** moving, directing

222: **expedition:** rapid journey or march

222: **Philippi:** Philippi is actually hundreds of miles away from Sardis, where Brutus's and Cassius's army is camped, yet the final battle does take place at Philippi; Shakespeare is compressing time and space for dramatic effect.

223: **of the selfsame tenor:** indicating the same

225: **proscription:** the statutes of outlawry employed by the triumvirate as an excuse to seize their enemies' property (see note 4.1.17)

BRUTUS
    Speak no more of her. Give me a bowl of wine.   210
    In this I bury all unkindness, Cassius.

                                           Drinks

CASSIUS
    My heart is thirsty for that noble pledge.
    Fill, Lucius, till the wine o'erswell the cup.
    I cannot drink too much of Brutus' love.

                               [Exit LUCIUS]
                 Enter TITINIUS with MESSALA

BRUTUS
    Come in, Titinius. Welcome, good Messala.   215
    Now sit we close about this taper here,
    And call in question our necessities.

CASSIUS
    Portia, art thou gone?

BRUTUS
                No more, I pray you.
    Messala, I have here received letters
    That young Octavius and Mark Antony   220
    Come down upon us with a mighty power,
    Bending their expedition toward Philippi.

MESSALA
    Myself have letters of the selfsame tenor.

BRUTUS
    With what addition?

MESSALA
    That by proscription and bills of outlawry   225
    Octavius, Antony, and Lepidus
    Have put to death an hundred senators.

233–247: It is unusual that Shakespeare would repeat the news of Portia's death here. It is likely that the playwright originally intended to omit this second announcement, but that the printer failed to observe the deletion. However, the two scenes can make sense in performance: a director can use the first instance to show Brutus's emotional vulnerability and the second to demonstrate his stoicism.

233: "Had you your letters from your wife, my lord?": Peter Jay Fernandez as Messala, Jamey Sheridan as Brutus, Dennis Boutsikaris as Cassius, and Ritchie Coster as Titinius in the Public Theater's 2000 production directed by Barry Edelstein
Photo: Michal Daniel

235: **writ of her:** have been written about her

237: **aught:** anything

BRUTUS
Therein our letters do not well agree.
Mine speak of seventy senators that died
By their proscriptions, Cicero being one.   230

CASSIUS
Cicero one?

MESSALA
                              Cicero is dead,
And by that order of proscription.
Had you your letters from your wife, my lord?

BRUTUS
No, Messala.

MESSALA
Nor nothing in your letters writ of her?   235

BRUTUS
Nothing, Messala.

MESSALA
                              That, methinks, is strange.

BRUTUS
Why ask you? Hear you aught of her in yours?

MESSALA
No, my lord.

BRUTUS
Now, as you are a Roman, tell me true.

MESSALA
Then like a Roman bear the truth I tell,   240
For certain she is dead, and by strange manner.

243: **once:** at some point

246: **this in art:** Stoical philosophy in principle

248: **to our work alive:** let us get back to the matter at hand

252: **waste his means:** use up their supplies

253: **offense:** harm

255: **of force:** necessarily

257: **affection:** allegiance

260: **a fuller number up:** i.e., new recruits

261: **new-added:** reinforced

BRUTUS
    Why, farewell, Portia. We must die, Messala.
    With meditating that she must die once,
    I have the patience to endure it now.

MESSALA
    Even so great men great losses should endure.   245

CASSIUS
    I have as much of this in art as you,
    But yet my nature could not bear it so.

BRUTUS
    Well, to our work alive. What do you think
    Of marching to Philippi presently?

CASSIUS
    I do not think it good.

BRUTUS
                  Your reason?

CASSIUS
                  This it is: 250
    'Tis better that the enemy seek us,
    So shall he waste his means, weary his soldiers,
    Doing himself offense, whilst we, lying still,
    Are full of rest, defense, and nimbleness.

BRUTUS
    Good reasons must, of force, give place to better.   255
    The people 'twixt Philippi and this ground
    Do stand but in a forced affection,
    For they have grudged us contribution.
    The enemy, marching along by them,
    By them shall make a fuller number up,   260
    Come on refreshed, new-added, and encouraged,
    From which advantage shall we cut him off,
    If at Philippi we do face him there,
    These people at our back.

265: **under your pardon:** I beg your pardon

272: **omitted:** missed

273: **bound in:** limited to

275: **serves:** is opportune

276: **ventures:** investments or enterprises, a phrase associated with merchants' sea trade

277: **along:** go

280: **niggard:** supply meagerly

282: **hence:** go hence, i.e., leave

CASSIUS
               Hear me, good brother.

BRUTUS
Under your pardon. You must note beside   265
That we have tried the utmost of our friends,
Our legions are brim-full, our cause is ripe.
The enemy increaseth every day;
We, at the height, are ready to decline.
There is a tide in the affairs of men,   270
Which, taken at the flood, leads on to fortune;
Omitted, all the voyage of their life
Is bound in shallows and in miseries.
On such a full sea are we now afloat,
And we must take the current when it serves   275
Or lose our ventures.

CASSIUS
             Then, with your will, go on;
We'll along ourselves and meet them at Philippi.

BRUTUS
The deep of night is crept upon our talk,
And nature must obey necessity,
Which we will niggard with a little rest.   280
There is no more to say?

CASSIUS
            No more. Good night.
Early tomorrow will we rise, and hence.

BRUTUS

Enter LUCIUS

Lucius, my gown.

[Exit LUCIUS]

           Farewell, good Messala.
Good night, Titinius. Noble, noble Cassius,
Good night and good repose.

291: **instrument:** referring to a stringed musical instrument

293: **knave:** lad

293: **o'erwatched:** tired from staying awake too long

Messala costume rendering from the May 28, 1957, staging by the Royal Shakespeare
Company at the Shakespeare Memorial Theatre directed by Glen Byam Shaw
Rare Book and Special Collections Library, University of Illinois at Urbana-Champaign

CASSIUS

            O my dear brother!   285
This was an ill beginning of the night.
Never come such division 'tween our souls!
Let it not, Brutus.

                        Enter LUCIUS with the gown

BRUTUS

            Everything is well.

CASSIUS

  Good night, my lord.

BRUTUS

            Good night, good brother.

TITINIUS *and* MESSALA

  Good night, Lord Brutus.

BRUTUS

            Farewell, everyone.   290
              Exeunt. [Manet BRUTUS and LUCIUS.]
Give me the gown. Where is thy instrument?

LUCIUS

  Here in the tent.

BRUTUS

            What, thou speak'st drowsily?
Poor knave, I blame thee not; thou art o'erwatched.
Call Claudio and some other of my men;
I'll have them sleep on cushions in my tent.   295

LUCIUS

  Varro and Claudio!

                      Enter VARRO and CLAUDIO

VARRO

  Calls my lord?

299: raise: wake

301: watch your pleasure: keep watch and be ready to carry out your wishes

303: otherwise bethink me: change my mind

308–309: "Canst thou hold up thy heavy eyes awhile / And touch thy instrument a strain or two?": Arthur Anderson as Lucius and Orson Welles as Brutus in the 1937–38 production directed by Orson Welles
© Condé Nast Archive/CORBIS

309: touch: play

310: an't: if it

313: might: ability

BRUTUS

    I pray you, sirs, lie in my tent and sleep.
    It may be I shall raise you by and by
    On business to my brother Cassius.   300

VARRO

    So please you, we will stand and watch your pleasure.

BRUTUS

    I will not have it so. Lie down, good sirs,
    It may be I shall otherwise bethink me.
    Look, Lucius, here's the book I sought for so,
    I put it in the pocket of my gown.   305
                          [VARRO and CLAUDIO lie down]

LUCIUS

    I was sure your lordship did not give it me.

BRUTUS

    Bear with me, good boy, I am much forgetful.
    Canst thou hold up thy heavy eyes awhile
    And touch thy instrument a strain or two?

LUCIUS

    Ay, my lord, an't please you.

BRUTUS

                  It does, my boy.   310
    I trouble thee too much, but thou art willing.

LUCIUS

    It is my duty, sir.

BRUTUS

    I should not urge thy duty past thy might;
    I know young bloods look for a time of rest.

LUCIUS

    I have slept, my lord, already.   315

Stage direction: Although Shakespeare calls only for music, Welles inserted a refrain of "Da dum de de dum" and twelve lines from Shakespeare's *Henry VIII* (3.1.3–14 in Bevington's Pearson Longman edition): "Orpheus with his lute made trees, / And mountain tops that freeze, / Bow themselves when he did sing. / To his music plants and flowers / Ever sprung, as sun and showers / There had made a lasting spring. / Everything that heard him play, / Even the billows of the sea, / Hung their heads, and then lay by. / In sweet music is such art, / Killing care and grief of heart / Fall asleep, or hearing, die."

319: **murderous slumber:** deep sleep (resembling death)

320: **mace:** refers to a sheriff's or bailiff's mace with which the official touched a person to signal their arrest

327: **how ill this taper burns:** (accepted sign of a ghost's appearance)

332: **stare:** stand up straight

336: "To tell thee thou shalt see me at Philippi": William Metzo as Julius Caesar's Ghost and Robert Cuccioli as Brutus in the Shakespeare Theatre of New Jersey's 2005 production directed by Brian B. Crowe
Photo: Gerry Goodstein

BRUTUS
 It was well done, and thou shalt sleep again;
 I will not hold thee long. If I do live,
 I will be good to thee.

                Music and a song

 This is a sleepy tune. O murderous slumber,
 Layest thou thy leaden mace upon my boy   320
 That plays thee music? Gentle knave, good night,
 I will not do thee so much wrong to wake thee.
 If thou dost nod, thou break'st thy instrument.
 I'll take it from thee; and, good boy, good night.
 Let me see, let me see, is not the leaf turned down   325
 Where I left reading? Here it is, I think.

        Enter the Ghost of CAESAR

 How ill this taper burns. Ha! Who comes here?
 I think it is the weakness of mine eyes
 That shapes this monstrous apparition.
 It comes upon me. Art thou anything?   330
 Art thou some god, some angel, or some devil,
 That mak'st my blood cold and my hair to stare?
 Speak to me what thou art.

GHOST
 Thy evil spirit, Brutus.

BRUTUS
 Why comest thou?   335

GHOST
 To tell thee thou shalt see me at Philippi.

BRUTUS
 Well, then I shall see thee again?

GHOST
 Ay, at Philippi.

Ghost of Caesar costume rendering from the May 28, 1957, staging by the Royal Shakespeare Company at the Shakespeare Memorial Theatre directed by Glen Byam Shaw

Rare Book and Special Collections Library, University of Illinois at Urbana-Champaign

343: **false:** out of tune

BRUTUS
Why, I will see thee at Philippi, then.

[Exit GHOST]   340

Now I have taken heart thou vanishest.
Ill spirit, I would hold more talk with thee.
Boy! Lucius! Varro! Claudio! Sirs, awake! Claudio!

LUCIUS
The strings, my lord, are false.

BRUTUS
He thinks he still is at his instrument.
Lucius, awake!   345

LUCIUS
My lord?

BRUTUS
Didst thou dream, Lucius, that thou so criedst out?

LUCIUS
My lord, I do not know that I did cry.

BRUTUS
Yes, that thou didst. Didst thou see anything?

LUCIUS
Nothing, my lord.   350

BRUTUS
Sleep again, Lucius. Sirrah Claudio!
Fellow, thou, awake!

VARRO
                    My lord?

CLAUDIUS
                              My lord?

357: **set on his powers:** advance his troops

357: **betimes:** early in the morning (without delay)

357: **before:** before us

Costume rendering for Brutus from the May 28, 1957, staging by the Royal Shakespeare
Company at the Shakespeare Memorial Theatre directed by Glen Byam Shaw
Rare Book and Special Collections Library, University of Illinois at Urbana-Champaign

BRUTUS

Why did you so cry out, sirs, in your sleep?

Both

Did we, my lord?

BRUTUS

Ay. Saw you anything?

VARRO

No, my lord, I saw nothing.

CLAUDIO

Nor I, my lord.   355

BRUTUS

Go and commend me to my brother Cassius.
Bid him set on his powers betimes before,
And we will follow.

Both

It shall be done, my lord.

Exeunt

[Julius Caesar

Act 5

Location: the plains of Philippi

4: **battles:** forces, troops

5: **warn:** challenge

6: **answering before we do demand of them:** respond to us before we call them to battle

7: **I am in their bosoms:** I know what's in their hearts

8: **wherefore:** why

9: **visit other places:** be or go elsewhere

10: **fearful bravery:** bravery that inspires fear

10: **face:** mere appearance

11: **fasten in our thoughts:** convince us

14: **bloody sign:** battle signal, e.g., a red flag

16: **softly:** cautiously

19: **cross me in this exigent:** contradict me at this critical juncture

Enter OCTAVIUS, ANTONY, and their army

OCTAVIUS
Now, Antony, our hopes are answerèd.
You said the enemy would not come down,
But keep the hills and upper regions.
It proves not so; their battles are at hand;
They mean to warn us at Philippi here,   5
Answering before we do demand of them.

ANTONY
Tut, I am in their bosoms, and I know
Wherefore they do it. They could be content
To visit other places and come down
With fearful bravery, thinking by this face   10
To fasten in our thoughts that they have courage.
But 'tis not so.

Enter a MESSENGER

Messenger
                    Prepare you, generals,
The enemy comes on in gallant show.
Their bloody sign of battle is hung out,
And something to be done immediately.   15

ANTONY
Octavius, lead your battle softly on
Upon the left hand of the even field.

OCTAVIUS
Upon the right hand I; keep thou the left.

ANTONY
Why do you cross me in this exigent?

Brutus, Cassius, and their army in the 1970 movie directed by Stuart Burge
Courtesy: Douglas Lanier

20: **do so:** do what I said

24: **we will answer on their charge:** we will counterattack when they charge

25: **make forth:** march forward

Scene: John Gielgud remembers how self-conscious Marlon Brando was in playing Antony, yet how open he was to constructive criticism. Discussing the one scene in which the film's biggest stars appear together, Gielgud writes, "We went through the speeches in the morning and he asked me, 'What did you think of the way I did those speeches?' So I went through them with him and made some suggestions. He thanked me very politely and went away. The next morning, when we shot the scene, I found that he had taken note of everything I had said and spoke the lines exactly as I had suggested."

OCTAVIUS
I do not cross you, but I will do so.   20

March. Drum.
Enter BRUTUS, CASSIUS, and their army
[: LUCILIUS, TITINIUS, MESSALA, and others.]

BRUTUS
They stand and would have parley.

CASSIUS
Stand fast, Titinius, we must out and talk.

OCTAVIUS
Mark Antony, shall we give sign of battle?

ANTONY
No, Caesar, we will answer on their charge.
Make forth, the generals would have some words.   25

OCTAVIUS
Stir not until the signal.

BRUTUS
Words before blows; is it so, countrymen?

OCTAVIUS
Not that we love words better, as you do.

BRUTUS
Good words are better than bad strokes, Octavius.

ANTONY
In your bad strokes, Brutus, you give good words.   30
Witness the hole you made in Caesar's heart,
Crying, "Long live! Hail, Caesar!"

33: **posture of your blows:** how you will strike

34: **Hybla:** a part of Sicily famous for its honey

38: **threat:** threaten

41: **showed your teeth:** smiled

47: **If Cassius might have ruled:** (Cassius recommends killing Antony at 2.1.155–57)

48: **the cause:** the business at hand

49: **the proof of it:** its trial (by sword)

51: **goes up:** will be put into the scabbard

53: **another Caesar:** referring to himself, Octavius

54: **have added slaughter:** has also been slaughtered

CASSIUS

                Antony,
The posture of your blows are yet unknown;
But, for your words, they rob the Hybla bees
And leave them honeyless.

ANTONY

                Not stingless too?   35

BRUTUS

  O, yes, and soundless too,
For you have stolen their buzzing, Antony,
And very wisely threat before you sting.

ANTONY

  Villains, you did not so, when your vile daggers
  Hacked one another in the sides of Caesar.   40
  You showed your teeth like apes, and fawned like hounds,
  And bowed like bondmen, kissing Caesar's feet,
  Whilst damnèd Casca, like a cur, behind
  Struck Caesar on the neck. O you flatterers!

CASSIUS

  Flatterers? Now, Brutus, thank yourself.   45
  This tongue had not offended so today
  If Cassius might have ruled.

OCTAVIUS

  Come, come, the cause. If arguing make us sweat,
  The proof of it will turn to redder drops.
  Look, I draw a sword against conspirators.   50
  When think you that the sword goes up again?
  Never, till Caesar's three and thirty wounds
  Be well avenged, or till another Caesar
  Have added slaughter to the sword of traitors.

BRUTUS

  Caesar, thou canst not die by traitors' hands   55
  Unless thou bring'st them with thee.

58: **strain:** lineage

60: **peevish schoolboy:** i.e., Octavius (peevish = silly; Octavius was eighteen at this point)

60: **worthless:** unworthy

61: **masker and a reveler:** pejorative references to Antony

65: **stomachs:** appetite (for the fight)

67: **on the hazard:** at risk

Octavius costume rendering from the May 28, 1957, staging by the Royal Shakespeare Company at the Shakespeare Memorial Theatre directed by Glen Byam Shaw

Rare Book and Special Collections Library, University of Illinois at Urbana-Champaign

OCTAVIUS
                    So I hope.
    I was not born to die on Brutus' sword.

BRUTUS
    O, if thou wert the noblest of thy strain,
    Young man, thou couldst not die more honorable.

CASSIUS
    A peevish schoolboy, worthless of such honor,   60
    Joined with a masker and a reveler!

ANTONY
    Old Cassius still.

OCTAVIUS
                    Come, Antony, away.—
    Defiance, traitors, hurl we in your teeth.
    If you dare fight today, come to the field;
    If not, when you have stomachs.   65
                    Exeunt OCTAVIUS, ANTONY, and their army

CASSIUS
    Why, now, blow wind, swell billow and swim bark.
    The storm is up, and all is on the hazard.

BRUTUS
    Ho, Lucilius, hark, a word with you.
                    LUCILIUS and MESSALA stand forth

LUCILIUS
    My lord.

                    [BRUTUS and LUCILIUS converse, apart]

CASSIUS
    Messala.

MESSALA
                    What says my general?

71: **as:** a redundancy used when expressing time

74: **Pompey was:** at the battle of Pharsalus, Pompey wanted to avoid battle with Caesar, but he gave into his eager troops and was defeated

74: **set:** risk

76: **Epicurus:** Epicureans did not believe in omens

78: **things that presage:** i.e., omens

79: **former ensign:** foremost standard (banner)

82: **consorted:** accompanied

84: **ravens, crows and kites:** all these scavengers were considered ill omens

86: **as:** as if

87: **fatal:** ominous

91: **very constantly:** with determination, unwaveringly

Scene: In Mankiewicz's film, numerous Roman foot soldiers and horsemen circle Gielgud and Mason to witness Cassius's and Brutus's farewell speech. The effect is oddly theatrical, almost as if they were watching a performance in the round.

93: **The gods today stand friendly:** may the gods favor us

94: **lovers:** close friends

95: **rest still:** remain always

CASSIUS
                    Messala,   70
This is my birthday, as this very day
Was Cassius born. Give me thy hand, Messala.
Be thou my witness that against my will,
As Pompey was, am I compelled to set
Upon one battle all our liberties.   75
You know that I held Epicurus strong
And his opinion. Now I change my mind,
And partly credit things that do presage.
Coming from Sardis, on our former ensign
Two mighty eagles fell, and there they perched,   80
Gorging and feeding from our soldiers' hands,
Who to Philippi here consorted us.
This morning are they fled away and gone,
And in their steads do ravens, crows and kites
Fly o'er our heads and downward look on us   85
As we were sickly prey. Their shadows seem
A canopy most fatal, under which
Our army lies, ready to give up the ghost.

MESSALA
Believe not so.

CASSIUS
                    I but believe it partly,
For I am fresh of spirit and resolved   90
To meet all perils very constantly.

BRUTUS
Even so, Lucilius.   *[Advances]*

CASSIUS
                    Now, most noble Brutus,
The gods today stand friendly, that we may,
Lovers in peace, lead on our days to age.
But since the affairs of men rest still incertain,   95
Let's reason with the worst that may befall.
If we do lose this battle, then is this
The very last time we shall speak together.
What are you then determinèd to do?

100: **that philosophy:** referring to Platonism

Charles Doran as Brutus, circa 1900
Courtesy: Harry Rusche

101: **Cato:** Brutus's father-in-law; see note 2.1.295

104: **fall:** occur, befall

104: **prevent:** cut short, anticipate

105: **time of life:** length of years, i.e., natural lifespan

106: **stay:** await

108: **triumph:** triumphs, in which the vanquished were paraded through Rome, were typically reserved for defeated foreign powers

109: **thorough:** through

112: **He bears too great a mind:** i.e., it would be too much (for Brutus) to bear

123: **ere:** before

BRUTUS

Even by the rule of that philosophy   100
By which I did blame Cato for the death
Which he did give himself—I know not how,
But I do find it cowardly and vile,
For fear of what might fall, so to prevent
The time of life—arming myself with patience   105
To stay the providence of some high powers
That govern us below.

CASSIUS

                    Then, if we lose this battle,
You are contented to be led in triumph
Thorough the streets of Rome?

BRUTUS

No, Cassius, no. Think not, thou noble Roman,   110
That ever Brutus will go bound to Rome.
He bears too great a mind. But this same day
Must end that work the ides of March begun,
And whether we shall meet again I know not.
Therefore our everlasting farewell take.   115
Forever and forever, farewell, Cassius.
If we do meet again, why, we shall smile;
If not, why then, this parting was well made.

CASSIUS

Forever and forever, farewell, Brutus.
If we do meet again, we'll smile indeed;   120
If not, 'tis true this parting was well made.

BRUTUS

Why, then, lead on. O, that a man might know
The end of this day's business ere it come!
But it sufficeth that the day will end,
And then the end is known. Come ho, away!   125

                                                    Exeunt

Location: on the battlefield at Philippi

Scene: John Houseman writes of the battle scene in the 1953 film: "It was an ambush in the best Western style, with Antony's men (in the Indian role) perched high in the hill above Bronson Canyon and Brutus and Cassius (the U.S. Cavalry) coming through the Pass, totally unaware of the fate that awaited them. We had about two hundred men in Brutus's army, including several dozen on horseback, and less than fifty with Antony. With intercutting between the unsuspecting horsemen below and Brando's grim, impassive Indian profile as he looked down at his prey, a certain tension was created that we stretched to the breaking point. The final charge and the 'battle' itself—fortified with rebel yells and much clanging of hardware on the sound track—was perfunctory to say the least."

1: **bills:** orders

3: **set on:** attack

4: **cold demeanor:** weak fighting spirit

4: **wing:** side

5: **overthrow:** defeat

Act 5, Scene 2]

Alarum. Enter BRUTUS and MESSALA.

BRUTUS
Ride, ride, Messala, ride, and give these bills
Unto the legions on the other side.

Loud alarum

Let them set on at once, for I perceive
But cold demeanor in Octavius' wing,
And sudden push gives them the overthrow.   5
Ride, ride, Messala, let them all come down.

Exeunt

Location: elsewhere on the battlefield

1: **villains:** i.e., Cassius's own troops

3: **ensign:** standard-bearer

4: **it:** the standard

6: **on:** over

7: **fell to spoil:** began to loot

11: **far:** farther

Alarums. Enter CASSIUS and TITINIUS.

CASSIUS
    O, look, Titinius, look, the villains fly!
    Myself have to mine own turned enemy.
    This ensign here of mine was turning back;
    I slew the coward and did take it from him.

TITINIUS
    O Cassius, Brutus gave the word too early,   5
    Who, having some advantage on Octavius,
    Took it too eagerly. His soldiers fell to spoil,
    Whilst we by Antony are all enclosed.

Enter PINDARUS

PINDARUS
    Fly further off, my lord, fly further off!
    Mark Antony is in your tents, my lord.   10
    Fly, therefore, noble Cassius, fly far off!

CASSIUS
    This hill is far enough. Look, look, Titinius,
    Are those my tents where I perceive the fire?

TITINIUS
    They are, my lord.

CASSIUS
               Titinius, if thou lovest me,
    Mount thou my horse and hide thy spurs in him   15
    Till he have brought thee up to yonder troops
    And here again that I may rest assured
    Whether yond troops are friend or enemy.

19: **even with a thought:** as fast as thought

21: **ever thick:** always blurred

21: **regard:** watch

22: **not'st:** note

23: **this day I breathèd first:** i.e., it is my birthday

23–50:
Orson Welles as Cassius, Erskine Sanford as Pindarus
John de Lancie as Cassius, Paul Winfield as Pindarus

tracks 40-42

25: **his compass:** its full circuit

29: **make to him on the spur:** approach him at full speed

31: **light:** dismount

38: **swore thee:** made you swear

38: **saving of:** sparing

40: **attempt:** do

TITINIUS
I will be here again, even with a thought.

Exit

CASSIUS
Go, Pindarus, get higher on that hill;   20
My sight was ever thick. Regard Titinius,
And tell me what thou not'st about the field.

[Exit PINDARUS]

This day I breathèd first, time is come round,
And where I did begin, there shall I end.
My life is run his compass. Sirrah, what news?   25

PINDARUS
(Above) O my lord!

CASSIUS
What news?

PINDARUS
Titinius is enclosèd round about
With horsemen that make to him on the spur,
Yet he spurs on. Now they are almost on him.   30
Now, Titinius! Now some light. O, he lights too.
He's ta'en.

Shout

And, hark! they shout for joy.

CASSIUS
Come down, behold no more.
O, coward that I am, to live so long,
To see my best friend ta'en before my face.   35

Enter PINDARUS

Come hither, sirrah.
In Parthia did I take thee prisoner,
And then I swore thee, saving of thy life,
That whatsoever I did bid thee do,
Thou shouldst attempt it. Come now, keep thine oath.   40
Now be a freeman, and with this good sword

tracks 40-42

23–50:
Orson Welles as Cassius, Erskine Sanford as Pindarus
John de Lancie as Cassius, Paul Winfield as Pindarus

42: **search:** probe

43: **stand not to answer:** do not delay by answering

45–46: "Caesar, thou art revenged, / Even with the sword that killed thee": David Arsenault as Pindarus and Richard Topol as Cassius in the Shakespeare Theatre of New Jersey's 2005 production directed by Brian B. Crowe
Photo: Gerry Goodstein

47: **so:** thus, by this act

48: **durst I:** if I had dared

51: **but change:** an even exchange

That ran through Caesar's bowels, search this bosom.
Stand not to answer. Here, take thou the hilts,
And, when my face is covered, as 'tis now,
Guide thou the sword.

[PINDARUS stabs him]

              Caesar, thou art revenged,   45
Even with the sword that killed thee.

[CASSIUS dies]

PINDARUS
    So, I am free, yet would not so have been
    Durst I have done my will. O Cassius,
    Far from this country Pindarus shall run,
    Where never Roman shall take note of him.   50

[Exit]
Enter TITINIUS with MESSALA

MESSALA
    It is but change, Titinius, for Octavius
    Is overthrown by noble Brutus' power,
    As Cassius' legions are by Antony.

TITINIUS
    These tidings will well comfort Cassius.

MESSALA
    Where did you leave him?

TITINIUS
              All disconsolate,   55
    With Pindarus his bondman, on this hill.

MESSALA
    Is not that he that lies upon the ground?

TITINIUS
    He lies not like the living. O my heart!

60: **O setting sun:** merely an exclamation, as Brutus states at 5.3.109 that it is three o'clock

65: **mistrust of my success:** doubts of my winning

66: **mistrust of good success:** doubts of our side winning

68: **apt:** impressionable

71: **mother:** i.e., melancholy (the melancholy person)

78: **hie:** hurry

80: **brave:** noble

Young Cato costume rendering from the May 28, 1957, staging by the Royal Shakespeare Company at the Shakespeare Memorial Theatre directed by Glen Byam Shaw

Rare Book and Special Collections Library, University of Illinois at Urbana-Champaign

MESSALA
    Is not that he?

TITINIUS
                    No, this was he, Messala,
    But Cassius is no more. O setting sun,   60
    As in thy red rays thou dost sink tonight,
    So in his red blood Cassius' day is set.
    The sun of Rome is set! Our day is gone;
    Clouds, dews, and dangers come. Our deeds are done.
    Mistrust of my success hath done this deed.   65

MESSALA
    Mistrust of good success hath done this deed.
    O hateful error, melancholy's child,
    Why dost thou show to the apt thoughts of men
    The things that are not? O error, soon conceived,
    Thou never com'st unto a happy birth,   70
    But kill'st the mother that engendered thee!

TITINIUS
    What, Pindarus? Where art thou, Pindarus?

MESSALA
    Seek him, Titinius, whilst I go to meet
    The noble Brutus, thrusting this report
    Into his ears. I may say thrusting it,   75
    For piercing steel and darts envenomèd
    Shall be as welcome to the ears of Brutus
    As tidings of this sight.

TITINIUS
                    Hie you, Messala,
    And I will seek for Pindarus the while.

                                        [Exit MESSALA]

    Why didst thou send me forth, brave Cassius?   80
    Did I not meet thy friends, and did not they
    Put on my brows this wreath of victory,
    And bid me give it thee? Didst thou not hear their shouts?

85: **hold thee:** wait

87: **apace:** quickly

88: **regarded:** found (and honored)

89: **a Roman's part:** i.e., suicide (By committing suicide, he denies his enemy
the opportunity to vanquish him and thus dies with honor, a Roman ideal.)

96: **proper:** own (the redundancy adds emphasis)

97: **whe'er he have not:** how he has (whe'er = whether)

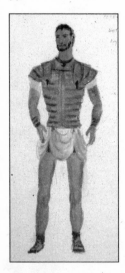

Strato costume rendering from the May 28, 1957, staging by the Royal Shakespeare
Company at the Shakespeare Memorial Theatre directed by Glen Byam Shaw
Rare Book and Special Collections Library, University of Illinois at Urbana-Champaign

Alas, thou hast misconstrued everything.
But hold thee, take this garland on thy brow.   85
Thy Brutus bid me give it thee, and I
Will do his bidding. Brutus, come apace,
And see how I regarded Caius Cassius.
By your leave, gods. This is a Roman's part.
Come, Cassius' sword, and find Titinius' heart.   90

Titinius dies
Alarum
Enter BRUTUS, MESSALA, YOUNG CATO,
STRATO, VOLUMNIUS, and LUCILIUS

BRUTUS
Where, where, Messala, doth his body lie?

MESSALA
Lo, yonder, and Titinius mourning it.

BRUTUS
Titinius' face is upward.

CATO
                    He is slain.

BRUTUS
O Julius Caesar, thou art mighty yet.
Thy spirit walks abroad and turns our swords   95
In our own proper entrails.

Low alarums

CATO
                    Brave Titinius!
Look, whe'er he have not crowned dead Cassius!

103: Kemble deleted this line, presumably to maintain his stern and stoic vision of Brutus by reducing sentiment whenever possible.

104: **Thasos:** an island near Philippi

106: **discomfort:** discourage

109: **ere:** before

Volumnius costume rendering from the May 28, 1957, staging by the Royal Shakespeare Company at the Shakespeare Memorial Theatre directed by Glen Byam Shaw

Rare Book and Special Collections Library, University of Illinois at Urbana-Champaign

BRUTUS
    Are yet two Romans living such as these?
    The last of all the Romans, fare thee well.
    It is impossible that ever Rome   100
    Should breed thy fellow. Friends, I owe mo tears
    To this dead man than you shall see me pay.
    I shall find time, Cassius, I shall find time.
    Come, therefore, and to Thasos send his body.
    His funerals shall not be in our camp,   105
    Lest it discomfort us. Lucilius, come,
    And come, young Cato, let us to the field.
    Labeo and Flavius, set our battles on.
    'Tis three o'clock, and, Romans, yet ere night
    We shall try fortune in a second fight.   110
                             Exeunt

Location: elsewhere on the battlefield

Lewis Waller as Brutus in Herbert Beerbohm Tree's production, circa 1900
Courtesy: Harry Rusche

2: **What bastard doth not?:** Who is of such low birth that he does not do so?

13: **Only I yield to die:** I yield only that I may die

14: **There is . . . kill me straight: 1)** There is much honor in killing me, Brutus, that you will execute me immediately **2)** Take this money and kill me at once

Act 5, Scene 4]

Alarum. Enter BRUTUS, MESSALA, [YOUNG] CATO,
LUCILIUS, [and] FLAVIUS.

BRUTUS
 Yet, countrymen, O, yet hold up your heads.
      [Exit BRUTUS, MESSALA, and FLAVIUS]

CATO
 What bastard doth not? Who will go with me?
 I will proclaim my name about the field.
 I am the son of Marcus Cato, ho!
 A foe to tyrants and my country's friend.   5
 I am the son of Marcus Cato, ho!
 Enter Soldiers and fight.

LUCILIUS
 And I am Brutus, Marcus Brutus, I!
 Brutus, my country's friend. Know me for Brutus!
       [YOUNG CATO is killed.]
 O young and noble Cato, art thou down?   10
 Why, now thou diest as bravely as Titinius,
 And mayst be honored, being Cato's son.

FIRST SOLDIER
 Yield, or thou diest.

LUCILIUS
     Only I yield to die.
 There is so much that thou wilt kill me straight
 Kill Brutus, and be honored in his death.   15

FIRST SOLDIER
 We must not. A noble prisoner!
            Enter ANTONY

25: **or alive:** either alive

26: **like himself:** true to himself

33: **is chanced:** has turned out

SECOND SOLDIER
　Room, ho! Tell Antony, Brutus is ta'en.

FIRST SOLDIER
　I'll tell the news. Here comes the general.
　Brutus is ta'en, Brutus is ta'en, my lord.

ANTONY
　Where is he?　　　　　　　　　　　　　　　　　20

LUCILIUS
　Safe, Antony, Brutus is safe enough.
　I dare assure thee that no enemy
　Shall ever take alive the noble Brutus.
　The gods defend him from so great a shame.
　When you do find him, or alive or dead,　　　25
　He will be found like Brutus, like himself.

ANTONY
　This is not Brutus, friend, but, I assure you,
　A prize no less in worth. Keep this man safe,
　Give him all kindness. I had rather have
　Such men my friends than enemies. Go on,　　30
　And see whe'er Brutus be alive or dead,
　And bring us word unto Octavius' tent
　How everything is chanced.

　　　　　　　　　　　　　　　　　　　Exeunt

Location: elsewhere on the field

Frank Benson as Brutus, circa 1905
Courtesy: Harry Rusche

2–3: showed the torchlight . . . not back: Plutarch describes Statilius carrying out a nighttime reconnaissance mission and giving Brutus an all's-well signal with a torch, but he was killed by the enemy when returning to Brutus's position.

5: deed in fashion: a common occurrence

Act 5, Scene 5]

Enter BRUTUS, DARDANIUS, CLITUS,
STRATO, and VOLUMNIUS

BRUTUS
Come, poor remains of friends, rest on this rock.

CLITUS
Statilius showed the torchlight, but, my lord,
He came not back. He is or ta'en or slain.

BRUTUS
Sit thee down, Clitus. Slaying is the word,
It is a deed in fashion. Hark thee, Clitus.   5

[Whispers]

CLITUS
What, I, my lord? No, not for all the world.

BRUTUS
Peace then, no words.

CLITUS
                              I'll rather kill myself.

BRUTUS
Hark thee, Dardanius.

                                                        [Whispers]

DARDANIUS
                              Shall I do such a deed?

CLITUS
O Dardanius!

18: **several:** separate

23: **the pit:** (hunted animals were driven into pits)

Dardanius costume rendering from the May 28, 1957, staging by the Royal Shakespeare Company at the Shakespeare Memorial Theatre directed by Glen Byam Shaw

Rare Book and Special Collections Library, University of Illinois at Urbana-Champaign

DARDANIUS
    O Clitus!   10

CLITUS
    What ill request did Brutus make to thee?

DARDANIUS
    To kill him, Clitus. Look, he meditates.

CLITUS
    Now is that noble vessel full of grief,
    That it runs over even at his eyes.

BRUTUS
    Come hither, good Volumnius, list a word.   15

VOLUMNIUS
    What says my lord?

BRUTUS
                        Why, this, Volumnius:
    The ghost of Caesar hath appeared to me
    Two several times by night, at Sardis once,
    And, this last night, here in Philippi fields.
    I know my hour is come.

VOLUMNIUS
                        Not so, my lord.   20

BRUTUS
    Nay, I am sure it is, Volumnius.
    Thou seest the world, Volumnius, how it goes.
    Our enemies have beat us to the pit.

                                                    Low alarums

    It is more worthy to leap in ourselves
    Than tarry till they push us. Good Volumnius,   25
    Thou know'st that we two went to school together.
    Even for that our love of old, I prithee,
    Hold thou my sword hilts, whilst I run on it.

29: **an office:** a job

tracks 43-45

31–51 and 67–74:
John Bowe and Adrian Lester
Patrick Wymark and Peter Finch

34: **joy:** rejoice

38: **vile:** ignoble, insignificant

39: **at once:** all at once

43: As part of his ruthless cutting of Act 5, Welles blacked out the stage on this line. Shafts of light then shone up from the floor revealing Antony, accompanied by storm troopers carrying large black banners, standing over the dead Brutus. With the audience's eyes fixed on the menacing image that underscored one last time Welles's anti-Fascist message, Antony spoke his final eight lines to bring the performance to an end.

45: **respect:** reputation

46: **smatch:** touch

VOLUMNIUS
That's not an office for a friend, my lord.

Alarum still

CLITUS
Fly, fly, my lord! There is no tarrying here.   30

BRUTUS
Farewell to you, and you, and you, Volumnius.
Strato, thou hast been all this while asleep;
Farewell to thee too, Strato. Countrymen,
My heart doth joy that yet in all my life
I found no man but he was true to me.   35
I shall have glory by this losing day
More than Octavius and Mark Antony
By this vile conquest shall attain unto.
So fare you well at once, for Brutus' tongue
Hath almost ended his life's history.   40
Night hangs upon mine eyes, my bones would rest,
That have but laboured to attain this hour.
Alarum. Cry within, "Fly, fly, fly!"

CLITUS
Fly, my lord, fly.

BRUTUS
Hence! I will follow.
[Exeunt CLITUS, DARDANIUS, and VOLUMNIUS]
I prithee, Strato, stay thou by thy lord.
Thou art a fellow of a good respect;   45
Thy life hath had some smatch of honor in it.
Hold then my sword, and turn away thy face
While I do run upon it. Wilt thou, Strato?

STRATO
Give me your hand first. Fare you well, my lord.

31–51 and 67–74:
John Bowe and Adrian Lester
Patrick Wymark and Peter Finch

51: When Kemble died as Brutus, the actors placed a laurel wreath on his head, and forty-two actors gathered around him for Antony's eulogy. Ironically, the image was reminiscent of the display surrounding Caesar in his death, though it is doubtful that Kemble would have wanted to draw such a comparison between his idealized, stoical patriot Brutus and his tyrannical Caesar. In contrast to the solemnity of Kemble's display, Edwin Booth sought a raw emotional response to his dying Brutus when, hearing a trumpet calling, he struggles in vain to rejoin the battle.

55: **make a fire of him:** cremate him

56: **only:** alone

60: **entertain them:** take them into service

62: **prefer:** recommend

60: "All that served Brutus, I will entertain them": Keith Hamilton Cobb as Octavius Caesar with the cast in the Shakespeare Theatre Company's 1993–94 production directed by Joe Dowling

Photo: Richard Anderson

BRUTUS

    Farewell, good Strato—*[Runs on his sword]*
                   Caesar, now be still,   50
    I killed not thee with half so good a will.

                                      Brutus dies.
        Alarum. Retreat. Enter ANTONY, OCTAVIUS,
            MESSALA, LUCILIUS, and the army.

OCTAVIUS

    What man is that?

MESSALA

    My master's man. Strato, where is thy master?

STRATO

    Free from the bondage you are in, Messala.
    The conquerors can but make a fire of him,   55
    For Brutus only overcame himself,
    And no man else hath honor by his death.

LUCILIUS

    So Brutus should be found. I thank thee, Brutus,
    That thou hast proved Lucilius' saying true.

OCTAVIUS

    All that served Brutus, I will entertain them.   60
    Fellow, wilt thou bestow thy time with me?

STRATO

    Ay, if Messala will prefer me to you.

OCTAVIUS

    Do so, good Messala.

MESSALA

                How died my master, Strato?

STRATO

    I held the sword and he did run on it.

tracks 43-45

31–51 and 67–74:
John Bowe and Adrian Lester
Patrick Wymark and Peter Finch

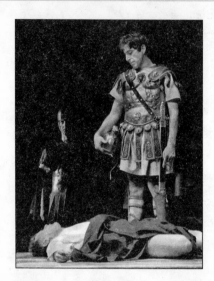

67: "This was the noblest Roman of them all": Al Pacino as Mark Antony in the Public Theater's 1987–88 production directed by Stuart Vaughan
Photo: George E. Joseph

70–71: **in a general . . . good to all:** with a genuine belief in the common good (general = selfless)

72: **gentle:** noble

75: **use:** treat

78: **ordered:** treated

79: **the field to rest:** an end to the fight

80: **part:** divide

80: **happy:** fortunate

MESSALA

    Octavius, then take him to follow thee,   65
    That did the latest service to my master.

ANTONY

    This was the noblest Roman of them all.
    All the conspirators save only he
    Did that they did in envy of great Caesar.
    He only, in a general honest thought   70
    And common good to all, made one of them.
    His life was gentle, and the elements
    So mixed in him that Nature might stand up
    And say to all the world, "This was a man."

OCTAVIUS

    According to his virtue, let us use him   75
    With all respect and rites of burial.
    Within my tent his bones tonight shall lie,
    Most like a soldier, ordered honorably.
    So call the field to rest, and let's away
    To part the glories of this happy day.   80

Exeunt

The Cast Speaks

Marie Macaisa

In the text of a Shakespeare play, directors, actors, and other interpreters of Shakespeare's work find a wealth of information. A hallmark of Shakespeare's writing is to tell us more than we need to know about a particular character, more than is needed to understand the plot. For example, in Cassius, we are given a myriad of motivations for Caesar's assassination: Cassius is a patriot and is acting for the good of Rome; he hates Caesar and is jealous of him; he is ambitious and is acting in his own interest, fueled by his ego. Yet, despite the spate of reasons, we remain very much uncertain of his primary motivation, an uncertainty that could have been settled had Shakespeare included the following line from his primary source for the play, Plutarch's *The Lives of Noble Grecians and Romans:* "But Cassius being a choleric man and hating Caesar privately, more than he did the tyranny openly." [Spevack, Marvin. *Julius Caesar,* The New Cambridge Shakespeare. 1988.]

While providing extra information, Shakespeare (like all playwrights and unlike novelists) also leaves gaps. We are thus coaxed to fill in the missing information ourselves, either through reasonable surmises (we can guess that Gertrude and Claudius were attracted to each other before Old Hamlet died) or through back stories we supply on our own (the idea that Mercutio was disappointed in love, not present in the text, to explain his attitude). This mix, simultaneously knowing too much and not enough about the characters, enable us to paint vivid, varied interpretations of the same play.

In staging a play, directors create a vision for their production starting from the text but also moving beyond the text by making decisions on what isn't in it. In collaboration with actors, they flesh out the characters: they discuss what they might be like, they create stories that explain their actions, they determine motivations, and they speculate on the nature of their relationships. In Shakespeare they have a rich text to draw on and hundreds of years of performances for inspiration. Thus we, the audience, can experience a play anew each time we see a different production: perhaps it is in an unfamiliar setting, perhaps it is in a scene or characterization we hadn't noticed in the past, perhaps it is in the realization that we have changed our opinions about the actions of the characters in the play. Would his enormous power have turned Caesar into a tyrant? Were the conspirators justified in their actions? Was Mark Antony right in calling Brutus "the noblest Roman of them all"? Whatever the case, a closer look into one cast's interpretation creates an opportunity for us to make up our own minds about their stories and in the process, gain new insights, not just into a play hundreds of years old but quite possibly into ourselves.

THE SHAKESPEARE THEATRE OF NEW JERSEY, 2005

Artistic director Bonnie J. Monte says of this Julius Caesar*: "Being a Brian Crowe production, you'll want to pull your limbs and body parts in from the aisles." Indeed, soldiers and plebeians run up and down the aisles, actors declaim from the balcony, there is movement and sound everywhere. And blood. Crowe's production features a strong-willed Caesar, one who fights back as he is being stabbed, further enraging his assassins and increasing the violence in the scene. Yet, in the end, this Caesar dies of a broken heart. Seeing Brutus on the side of the conspirators, Caesar gives up and lets them kill him.*

These interviews were conducted in November 2005, toward the end of the run of the production. The actors were interviewed in groups and asked about their characters, their relationships, and a scene or two in which their character figures. Keep in mind that their answers represent but one interpretation of the play. You may be surprised; you may agree or disagree strongly with a point of view. That is exactly the point.

The play opens with two minor characters, Murellus and Flavius, immediately raising concerns on issues that recur throughout the play: the psychology of the mob mentality and the consequences of Caesar as an all-powerful, lone ruler.

Murellus: John Pieza

Murellus is a tribune, a representative of the people. He's in the very first scene, addressing some of the people celebrating Caesar's triumph over Pompey. He admonishes the crowd for their short memory, reminding them they used to cheer for Pompey and now here they are cheering for the man who defeated him. It is an important speech for launching the play and putting us in context. It also shows how easily the plebeians are swayed by whoever speaks to them.

Flavius: Jonathan Brathwaite

I play Flavius, another tribune. Together with Murellus, we reveal an unease, a distrust of Caesar gaining power and becoming a one-man ruler. Yes, Caesar came back as a valiant conqueror, but it was through civil war. We plant the seed of Caesar not really being trustworthy. We show that not everyone agrees with him, worships him.

Murellus: John Pieza

The fact that Flavius and Murellus are silenced brings up the fundamental question of what kind of man Caesar is. Can Caesar really be trusted with

Murellus (John Pieza) and Flavius (Jonathan Brathwaite) discuss Caesar's return
Photo by Gerry Goodstein

the ultimate power? All they do is they take down these things that are tributes to Caesar—they don't even post anything, incendiary or otherwise—and they're silenced for that! What is Caesar really capable of doing?

The Julius Caesar in this production is a strong-willed, formidable ruler, worthy of Antony's line, "Here was a Caesar. When comes such another?"

Julius Caesar: William Metzo

Caesar is a very powerful man, mindful of his legacy. He has returned to Rome triumphant, after destroying Pompey and defeating his armies. In his first scene, he expresses his desire to have a child by asking Antony to help "shake off their sterile curse." He wants to have a child, I believe, so that an heir of his can take over. If he dies without an heir and the senate takes over, they will rescind everything he did.

Brutus: Robert Cuccioli

I go with the rumor that exists that Brutus is Caesar's illegitimate son. It's not exactly in the text, but it's glanced at in a couple of places. When Caesar says, "Et tu, Brute?" it actually means, "And you, my child?" [*Ed. "Brute" is Brutus. However, in* The Twelve Caesars, *translated from* De vita Caesarum, *a work by the Roman biographer Suetonius, Caesar's last words were recorded as, "You too, my child?"*] And Brutus tells Antony after the assassination: "Our reasons are so full of good regard / That were you, Antony, the son of Caesar, / You should be satisfied." I found it beneficial to go with that assumption.

Both Brutus and Julius Caesar are married, and their relationships with their wives add nuances to their characterization. The private domesticity also provides a counterpoint to the very public political arena of the play. Both actors portray their characters as loving their wives deeply. Caesar, whose wife is much younger than he, wants to have a child with her. Brutus's wife might be pregnant. There is a reference to her "weak condition" in 2.1.

Calphurnia: Jessica Morris

When I was first cast, I was told I was going to play a trophy wife. I automatically assumed the relationship was not going to be a loving one. But the moment I started reading with Bill [William Metzo, who plays Julius Caesar], I realized it was just the opposite. Caesar was madly in love with her, totally enamored of her. Historically she was significantly younger than he was. Calphurnia was around twenty-three when Caesar was killed. Caesar was in his fifties.

In her first scene, it's become more and more obvious to me as the production has gone on that she's just been allowed into public life. She's still studying up on what she's supposed to do when she's taken out in public. She's learning, but she's very wide-eyed and inexperienced. I think she's thrilled Caesar is doing so well and it is all very exciting for her.

When Decius Brutus says, "The Senate have concluded / To give this day a crown to mighty Caesar," a couple of days ago that would have been wonderful news to her, but on this particular day, when she's feeling very suspicious and has had all these bad dreams, the announcement of the crown for her is not a good one. That scene is such a good clue about her character and her position. He and she have a private moment where he agrees with her, and then the second there is one other person on stage, then his public persona so strongly comes into play. He jokes around with the senators, almost at her expense. She's embarrassed. Bill would do things that were perfect, very appropriate for the scene—I got slapped on the butt one day, patted on the head, patted on the hand. It heightens Calphurnia's embarrassment and insecurity and reinforces her status in that society.

Portia: Roxanna Hope

There was a lot talk initially about Portia being crazy. After all, she walks in and has slashed herself in the thigh. I don't necessarily agree with that. What I see is someone who loves her husband very much; it's not a marriage of convenience ["By all your vows of love and that great vow / Which did incorporate and make us one"]. I found in Portia's language an attempt to match Brutus's, with his stoicism and nobility and idealism. But it also has an undercurrent of passion. What if she has spent her entire marriage trying to live up to those expectations, but underneath she just desperately loves her husband and wants this connection? I found support for that in the language. She comes in—we decided she was in the early stages of pregnancy ["It is not for your health thus to commit / Your weak condition to the raw cold morning"], she begins listing his behavior in the last couple of days. Everything that she voices is concern for him and his behavior towards her. She's not talking politics, war; she's talking about their relationship, his actions towards her, his distance.

This is someone who knows her husband. When she sees him unraveling, she starts to lose it. Every action she takes, she's been driven to. To slash her thigh—it's like suicide was then—is noble, a show of solidarity with him. It shows that she can be as strong as he needs her to be in order for him to confide in her. And the final plea with him wanting to be his other half, his soul mate, illustrates something very familiar, very domestic, that's about to be lost. That is something else to which the audience can relate.

Portia (Roxanna Hope) begs Brutus (Robert Cuccioli) to confide in her
Photo by Gerry Goodstein

Portia dies offstage, though I think the second time you see Portia, it's the beginning of her death. At that point, she knows she's going to lose Brutus and she's lost the battle with herself between being the honorable, silent, supportive wife and the frantic, passionate woman in love. She has rapidly begun to unravel. Also, her father having killed himself adds to her anxiety. She observes echoes of her father in Brutus and begins to feel so strongly that something terrible is going to happen. She's struggling mightily to keep it together. She doesn't sound crazy to me.

As noted by the actor playing Portia, Brutus struggles with his decision to join the conspiracy, but ultimately convinces himself to do it for the good of Rome. However, the motivations of the other conspirators: Cassius, Casca, Trebonius, Decius, Cinna, and Metellus Cimber, are not quite as clear. The actors, working with their director and informed by the text and by the performances of others in the cast, put forward their reasons for why their characters joined the conspiracy.

Brutus: Robert Cuccioli
Brutus is an idealist. He is hoping for the betterment of all. He also has a healthy ego and Cassius appeals to that. Brutus feels that he's necessary for this thing to work, after Caesar, so he talks himself into it. He convinces himself that Caesar is going to be a tyrant, and it starts making sense to him. It's not really the letter he receives [in 2.1]. Those kind of letters, for a person in Brutus's position, are like junk mail. He gets tons of them. Like he says, "Such instigations have been often dropped / Where I have took them up." There might be some underlying bitterness, with Caesar looking for an heir when he already has one.

Cassius: Richard Topol
Cassius thinks that Caesar is going to ruin the country. He has already ruined his life and the lives of everyone around him. In this production, clearly Caesar hates Cassius and doesn't allow him to have a say in the running of the government around him. Cassius believes, like many politicians, that what he thinks about the way the world should be is important and should be followed through. He's ambitious.

Cassius doesn't quite have the nerve to kill Caesar on his own though. He needs to have Brutus to be part of it and to say that it's the right thing to do. As he says to Casca, "Him and his worth and our great need of him." Cassius believes that if they have the guy whom everyone likes with them, then

Brutus (Robert Cuccioli) and Cassius (Richard Topol)
Photo by Gerry Goodstein

everyone will believe it's the right thing. He honors, respects, and loves Brutus and knows him much better than the other conspirators. Historically they were brothers-in-law.

Casca: Leon Addison Brown

There are as many questions about Casca as there are answers. His first big speech is an expository monologue about Caesar refusing the crown [1.1]. Who is he? He's not Brutus, not Cassius, not a warrior. He's a politician in Caesar's inner circle. He hates everything and everybody. I think he's one of these people who has a lot of things going on inside that he can't act on. He can't do what Caesar does, nor what Brutus does, nor what Cassius does. He's not that active in his personality and in his position. He envies Caesar. I would start with the fact that he's the biggest coward in the play. I would explore that aspect of him and build everything off that.

When he's talking to Cassius, he says, "Be factious for redress of all these griefs, / And I will set this foot of mine as far / As who goes farthest." In other words, if you do it, I'll do it. That's like when we were twelve years old. Each time I read him, something hits me differently.

I think he gets talked into the conspiracy because he doesn't like Caesar anyway. Caesar is everything he's not. It's about jealousy and envy. He never talks about the state. Who cares about the state? He's something Casca can't be.

Trebonius: John Pieza

Trebonius is a reluctant conspirator. He doesn't actually stab Caesar in the play; he's the one who gets Mark Antony out of the way. One of my favorite things about the conspirators is that there's very little written, outside Brutus and Cassius, about why they're doing it. It's a great thing for the actor because I get to make up a whole life and world. For me, Trebonius isn't idealistic, he's practical. He decides this is the bandwagon to get on. He realizes he'll never have the type of the power he should have under Caesar and that he'll never rise to his rightful place. In the script, there's not much that tells you about Trebonius's motivation and I get to fill in the blanks. Shakespeare gives you enough to develop your character.

In rehearsal and performance during preview week, Cassius says something to Mark Antony that I reacted to. He says, "Your voice shall be as strong as any man's / In the disposing of new dignities." And I looked at him like, "Where is that coming from? We never said that was going to be the case." And I thought to myself that's the key to Trebonius.

Decius Brutus: Raphael Peacock

Decius was a general. He excelled as a general and became very good friends with Caesar, so good that he is named heir. Therefore he is very well-aligned. However, he knows he needs to watch what's going on or wind up dead. I think he becomes a conspirator to watch everything. He knows that if Caesar is killed by Cassius, the will in which he is named heir won't matter and his own position becomes tenuous. He is there to keep an eye on everything and protect his place. He's willing for Brutus and Cassius to step forward, and I think if there were any way he could have gotten out of participating, he would have. But he really wanted to be part of whatever happened next.

Decius Brutus (Raphael Peacock) arrives to accompany Caesar (William Metzo) to the senate, much to Calphurnia's (Jessica Morris) dismay
Photo by Gerry Goodstein

Cinna: Tristan Colton

He was a real senator, Lucius Cornelius Cinna the Younger. He was also a Praetor, a higher senate member. In our production, he's a younger guy. There's not too much information in the text about him, so what we decided was that he is one of the younger senators, heavily influenced by Cassius and especially Brutus. He might have looked up to Brutus. One of my first lines is to Cassius about Brutus, "O Cassius, if you could / But win the noble Brutus to our party." He's also the errand boy and messenger of the group. He's sent to find people, he's charged with putting letters where Brutus might come upon it.

Like Brutus, he believes that it's the end of the senate if Caesar becomes king, and he wants to stop him. I do think he's jarred by the outcome, the actual killing. You never see him again after that. Once the conspirators leave the senate house, most of them are never heard from again. We don't know whether he ran away with the others or went to battle.

Metellus Cimber: Nathan Kaufman

Metellus Cimber speaks the least of the conspirators. He is the youngest and least experienced. He's very good in his job as a senator and that's why he's been asked to be part of this. He's an idealist, very proud of the Republic, and when he finds it to be threatened, he believes that the group of conspirators is best option. He doesn't really realize what he got himself into. From the idea of sacrificing a man to help save a nation and republic to when you actually sink a knife into human flesh is a long journey. And how that affects a human being is the story I tell.

Cicero: Geddeth Smith

Cicero is a distinguished senator. He moves the plot along in the scene with Casca by finding out from him that Caesar is coming to the Capitol tomorrow. He's not a conspirator, yet you're not really sure what Cicero is up to.

Two other characters, Artemidorus and the Soothsayer, attempt to warn Caesar of the danger to him.

Artemidorus: David Arsenault

I don't know how Artemidorus knows about the conspiracy in such great detail. In Isaac Asimov's *Guide to Shakespeare,* he says that Artemidorus was a professor of rhetoric and that he taught Cinna and Metellus Cimber. He was probably in the same room with them when they were gossiping about it. I think there must have been some murmur of gossip that he investigated himself to put the whole picture together. He seems to me extra nervous, so I don't know that he's one hundred percent certain that everything he knows is true. But he knows something is going to happen, he just isn't sure when. In this production, they drag him off the stage to kill him.

Soothsayer: Patrick Toon

There was a character that occurred in Italian Renaissance literature named Hermes Trismegistus, who was an Egyptian sage, a wise man, a holy man.

He pops up in other works and he helps out important people by giving them advice. I decided I would make the Soothsayer an incarnation of that character. We start the show with him casting the bones and seeing the omens about Caesar. In the end we do the same thing, with Mark Antony and Octavius in the background.

The assassination scene in this production was very graphic and violent. Caesar did not go down meekly; he swung at the conspirators; he fought back. Plebeians and soldiers were running up and down the aisles of the theater and the balcony, shouting. There was movement and sound all around.

Julius Caesar: William Metzo

In [the assassination] scene, the conspirators bait me. They know I admire courage and men who stand up for themselves, so they all grovel in front of me, get down on their knees, and kiss my feet, and it just drives me crazy. I just let loose on them all. They're being so unmanly in my eyes. Brutus sees me waxing superior and magnificent and that might have spurred him. [The conspirators] do it on purpose, I feel.

The conspirators hold Caesar down, right before they stab him
Photo by Gerry Goodstein

There are physical benefits from the action of groveling that came up in the choreography. You have two guys holding Caesar by the legs, one guy holding him by the arm, and it roots him, and so he becomes an easy target for Casca to get in the first strike. They can hold him steady for one moment.

We decided early in rehearsal that I would be strong and fight back. In fact it is only when I see that Brutus is on their side that I give up and allows them to kill me. Caesar dies of a broken heart rather than being overpowered.

Cassius: Richard Topol

We wanted to show in this scene why it was necessary for him to be killed. We begged him to be merciful to Publius Cimber and he's not; he is unyielding ["But I am constant as the Northern Star"]. We kill him in public in an effort to make it seem righteous. We want to get the people on our side. We know that kneeling before him will drive him out of his mind. We want to show the public how unbendable he is, what a tyrant he is.

Antony calls them on this in Act 5: "You showed your teeth like apes, and fawned like hounds, / And bowed like bondmen, kissing Caesar's feet, / Whilst damnèd Casca, like a cur, behind / Struck Caesar on the neck."

Mark Antony: Gregory Derelian

After the killing, Brutus, the idealist, explains to Mark Antony that it was for Rome that he acted ["And pity to the general wrong of Rome— / As fire drives out fire, so pity pity— / Hath done this deed on Caesar"]. Cassius's next line to me however is, "Your voice shall be as strong as any man's / In the disposing of new dignities." I take that as the reason he acted. As far as I'm concerned, that's why you would kill someone: for ambition or power.

My initial thought on Cassius is that he's not dangerous. He's a noble Roman, a good guy. But at the end of the assassination scene, when I am left with Caesar's body, Cassius is the last one to go and we look at each other, he with the bloody dagger in hand. That's when I realize I am in danger from him. Even though Brutus has told me that I was going to live.

Brutus: Robert Cuccioli:

Brutus thinks the best of every man all the time, and that's why he lets Antony live. And he believes the Romans will understand what they did and why that was the right thing.

Mark Antony: Gregory Derelian

Regarding the "Friends, Romans, Countrymen" speech [3.2], I don't think Antony planned it; I think it was off the cuff and comes out of the moment. He knew how valueless his life had become and that Cassius is watching him. Brutus is the only one keeping him alive. When he says, "I do beseech ye, if you bear me hard, / Now, whilst your purpled hands do reek and smoke, / Fulfil your pleasure," three guys make a move to kill him and Brutus stops them. Brutus has put tight conditions on the speech, and I imagined I had a guy standing three feet behind me, holding a knife.

Mark Antony incites the crowd with his oration. In this production, the plebeians listening to him wear masks, a scary realization of the mob mentality.

Plebeian #6: Jonathan Brathwaite

Regarding the Plebeians, the message here is that if you control the masses, you control Rome. All of us plebeians were given masks, from the nose up. The Soothsayer also has a mask but it is more extensive. The purpose of the mask is to give a singularity to the masses. It also adds mystery and danger, for example, in the scene where we kill Cinna the poet.

Artemidorus is dressed in rags and a mask. He represents the lowest tier of society, the most poor. You see in the costuming the hierarchy. We move through the plebeians, up to the senators, and then to Caesar and Calphurnia.

Cinna the poet: Geddeth Smith

The incident with Cinna the poet [3.3] is in Plutarch [Shakespeare's source for the play]. It is exactly what it portrays: common people can be dangerous.

After Caesar's death, a new triumvirate is formed to rule Rome: Mark Antony, Octavius Caesar, and Lepidus.

Mark Antony: Gregory Derelian

It's an uneasy alliance for the triumvirs after Caesar's death. Octavius and Antony need each other—Octavius is Caesar's heir and Antony has the crowd on his side. Octavius also has an army with him. Lepidus? Antony despises him. He considers him inept, too cautious, a bit of a politician. It wasn't his choice to bring him in. He asks, "Is it fit, / The threefold world divided, he should stand / One of the three to share it?"

Lepidus: Geddeth Smith

Lepidus, I think, is there to show that that triumvirate is in danger from the very beginning. Antony hates him, and he doesn't like the other two. He was a great general and potentially a very powerful one, otherwise, he wouldn't have been chosen. As we know, Antony doesn't survive but Lepidus does. He eventually dies in his bed.

Mark Antony: Gregory Derelian

That scene [4.1] is very telling. Antony, fresh from delivering a heroic oration and eulogizing Caesar is shown making a list of men they are condemning to die. Mark Antony's nephew is on the list, so is Lepidus's brother. It's a long list, and it's clear they've been at it for a while. You see Antony in a completely different light. The scene hints at the trouble ahead; as we know, this arrangement doesn't last long.

   The second half of the play, from Act 4 to the end, focuses on the battle between the new rulers and the armies of Brutus and Cassius. New characters are introduced and though they are small parts, the actors have carefully considered and developed ideas on how they fit within the story.

Pindarus: David Arsenault

Pindarus is a bondman [servant] who was previously taken prisoner. I like Pindarus a lot because even if he's a small part of the play, what he says has major consequences. What I see on the hill and how I misinterpret it is why Cassius kills himself. At first, I was playing that scene after Cassius's death [5.3.47] as fear. I was afraid someone would find me next to Cassius's body and assumed I killed him. As I played it a couple of times though, I began to realize that he was running away because he recognized the opportunity to become free. If he stuck around, at best someone else would take him as a servant. Running away seemed to be the only answer.

Titinius: Jonathan Brathwaite

Titinius is the right-hand man of Cassius and one of the highest-ranking generals in his army. I kill myself when I come upon him after he kills himself. Everything is lost, all hope is lost, the idea of what we wanted for Rome is lost. There's an aspect of idealism in the death and also respect—dying for my lord. Suicide was a noble way to go then. It also brings home the idea that we were willing to die for the cause.

Clitus: Nathan Kaufman

Clitus is one of Brutus's soldiers. In my mind, I rank him above a regular footman, but not yet at the same rank as Messala; he's working his way up. He's a very, very good soldier, and his mind is always in the game; he's always watching the field. I love my leader, Brutus, and it saddens me that he wants to die. Clitus is the person that Brutus first asks to kill him but he refuses. He's the kind of person who will not give up, but in the end, all is lost anyway.

Servant, Messenger: Monal Pathak

Bill [William Metzo, who plays Julius Caesar] and I decided during the table read that I was the illegitimate child of Caesar and Cleopatra. So I get interested when I hear that the senators are going to give mighty Caesar the crown. Am I next in line then?

I'm also the messenger who brings Antony the news that Brutus and Cassius are ready to fight. That gets the play moving forward. In the scene, there was a power struggle between Antony and Octavius. Octavius wants to grab the letter but Antony gets it first. We choreographed it such that when I came in, Antony was ready and Octavius was not.

Finally, the fates of Cassius and Brutus are decided; that of Mark Antony's is hinted at. The director of this production made the choice to have Caesar's ghost come back and witness much of the events at Philippi, including the suicides.

Cassius: Richard Topol

The relationship between Cassius and Brutus is one of the central relationships in the play: two brothers who make a fateful decision and how it ruins their country and themselves. I used to think the second half of the play, from Act 4 to the end, was not as well written or perhaps substantial as the first half. But the scenes in the second half with Brutus, the tent scene [4.2], is rich, deep, and textured in ways that were surprising.

Brutus: Robert Cuccioli

Both Cassius and Brutus kill themselves. Or rather, they have people help them with suicide. Cassius asks Pindarus to stab him, and I have Lucius hold the knife while I run into it. In the text of the play, it is Strato who does this, but we chose instead to have Lucius, my long-time servant, do this. He was with me at the beginning, and he's here with me now.

Brutus reasons that everything has fallen apart. There was no real plan about what was to happen to Rome after the assassination and the conspirators are now outcasts. His wife has killed herself, so has his best friend,

Octavius (Derek Wilson) picks up Brutus's sword as Mark Antony (Gregory Derelian) beholds Brutus's dead body
Photo by Gerry Goodstein

seventy to one hundred senators are dead, and most of all, he's killed some-one he loves. He realizes that he's made a tragic mistake and the only honor-able thing left for him is suicide. Brutus senses Caesar's presence when he kills himself.

Mark Antony: Gregory Derelian

The last scene of the play has Octavius picking up Brutus's sword and wip-ing the blood off it. In the meantime, Antony is crouched over Brutus's body. The handkerchief drops, and Antony looks up to see the sword pointed at him. Then the lights go down.

A Voice Coach's Perspective on Speaking Shakespeare

KEEPING SHAKESPEARE PRACTICAL

Andrew Wade

track 46-47

Introduction to Speaking Shakespeare: Derek Jacobi
Speaking Shakespeare: Andrew Wade with Drew Cortese

Why, you might be wondering, is it so important to keep Shakespeare practical? What do I mean by practical? Why is this the way to discover how to speak the text and understand it?

Plays themselves are not simply literary events—they demand interpreters in the deepest sense of the word, and the language of Shakespeare requires, therefore, not a vocal demonstration of writing techniques but an imaginative response to that writing. The key word here is imagination. The task of the voice coach is to offer relevant choices to the actor so that the actor's imagination is titillated, excited by the language, which he or she can then share with an audience, playing on that audience's imagination. Take the word "IF"—it is only composed of two letters when written, but if you say it aloud and listen to what it implies, then your reaction, the way the word plays through you, can change the perception of meaning. "Iffffffff"…you might hear and feel it implying "possibilities," "choices," "questioning," "trying to work something out." The saying of this word provokes active investigation of thought. What an apt word to launch a play: "If music be the food of love, play on" (Act 1, Scene 1 in *Twelfth Night, or What You Will*). How this word engages the listener and immediately sets up an involvement is about more than audibility. How we verbalize sounds has a direct link to meaning and understanding. In the words of Touchstone in *As You Like It*, "Much virtue in if."

I was working with a company in Vancouver on *Macbeth,* and at the end of the first week's rehearsal—after having explored our voices and opening out different pieces of text to hear the possibilities of the rhythm, feeling how the meter affects the thinking and feeling, looking at structure and form— one of the actors admitted he was also a writer of soap operas and that I had completely changed his way of writing. Specifically, in saying a line like, "The multitudinous seas incarnadine / Making the green one red" he heard the complexity of meaning revealed in the use of polysyllabic words becoming monosyllabic, layered upon the words' individual dictionary definitions. The writer was reminded that merely reproducing the speech of everyday life was nowhere near as powerful and effective as language that is shaped.

Do you think soap operas would benefit from rhyming couplets? Somehow this is difficult to imagine! But, the writer's comments set me thinking. As I am constantly trying to find ways of exploring the acting process, of opening out actors' connection with language that isn't their own, I thought it would be a good idea to involve writers and actors in some practical work on language. After talking to Cicely Berry (voice director, the Royal Shakespeare Company) and Colin Chambers (the then RSC production adviser), we put together a group of writers and actors who were interested in taking part. It was a fascinating experience all round, and it broke down barriers and misconceptions.

The actors discovered, for instance, that a writer is not coming from a very different place as they are in their creative search; that an idea or an image may result from a struggle to define a gut feeling and not from some crafted, well-formed idea in the head. The physical connection of language to the body was reaffirmed. After working with a group on Yeats's poem "Easter 1916," Ann Devlin changed the title of the play she was writing for the Royal Shakespeare Company to *After Easter*. She had experienced the poem read aloud by a circle of participants, each voice becoming a realization of the shape of the writing. Thus it made a much fuller impact on her and caused her thinking to shift. Such practical exchanges, through language work and voice, feed and stimulate my work to go beyond making sure the actors' voices are technically sound.

It is, of course, no different when we work on a Shakespeare play. A similar connection with the language is crucial. Playing Shakespeare, in many ways, is crafted instinct. The task is thus to find the best way to tap into someone's imagination. As Peter Brook put it: "People forget that a text is dumb. To make it speak, one must create a communication machine. A living network, like a nervous system, must be made if a text which comes from far away is to touch the sensibility of the present."

This journey is never to be taken for granted. It is the process that every text must undergo every time it is staged. There is no definitive rehearsal that would solve problems or indicate ways of staging a given play. Again, this is where creative, practical work on voice can help forge new meaning by offering areas of exploration and challenge. The central idea behind my work comes back to posing the question, "How does meaning change by speaking out aloud?" It would be unwise to jump hastily to the end process for, as Peter Brook says, "Shakespeare's words are records of the words that he wanted spoken, words issuing from people's mouths, with pitch, pause, and rhythm and gesture as part of their meaning. A word does not start as a word—it is the end product which begins as an impulse, stimulated by attitude and behavior which dictates the need for expression." (1)

PRACTICALLY SPEAKING

Something happens when we vocalize, when we isolate sounds, when we start to speak words aloud, when we put them to the test of our physicality, of our anatomy. We expose ourselves in a way that makes taking the language back more difficult. Our body begins a debate with itself, becomes alive with the vibrations of sound produced in the mouth or rooted deep in the muscles that aim at defining sound. In fact, the spoken words bring into play all the senses, before sense and another level of meaning are reached.

"How do I know what I think, until I see what I say," Oscar Wilde once said. A concrete illustration of this phrase was reported to me when I was leading a workshop recently. A grandmother said the work we had done that day reminded her of what her six-year-old grandson had said to his mother while they were driving through Wales: "Look, mummy, sheep! Sheep! Sheep!" "You don't have to keep telling us," the mother replied, but the boy said, "How do I know they're there, if I don't tell you?!"

Therefore, when we speak of ideas, of sense, we slightly take for granted those physical processes which affect and change their meaning. We tend to separate something that is an organic whole. In doing so, we become blind to the fact that it is precisely this physical connection to the words that enables the actors to make the language theirs.

The struggle for meaning is not just impressionistic theater mystique; it is an indispensable aspect of the rehearsal process and carries on during the life of every production. In this struggle, practical work on Shakespeare is vital and may help spark creativity and shed some light on the way meaning is born into language. After a performance of *More Words*, a show devised and directed by Cicely Berry and myself, Katie Mitchell (a former artistic director of The Other Place in Stratford-upon-Avon) gave me an essay by Ted Hughes that echoes with the piece. In it, Ted Hughes compares the writing of a poem—the coming into existence of words—to the capture of a wild animal. You will notice that in the following passage Hughes talks of "spirit" or "living parts" but never of "thought" or "sense." With great care and precaution, he advises, "It is better to call [the poem] an assembly of living parts moved by a single spirit. The living parts are the words, the images, the rhythms. The spirit is the life which inhabits them when they all work together. It is impossible to say which comes first, parts or spirit."

This is also true of life in words, as many are connected directly to one or several of our senses. Here Hughes talks revealingly of "the five senses," of "word," "action," and "muscle," all things which a practical approach to language is more likely to allow one to perceive and do justice to.

Words that live are those which we hear, like "click" or "chuckle," or which we see, like "freckled" or "veined," or which we taste, like "vinegar" or "sugar," or touch, like "prickle" or "oily," or smell, like "tar" or "onion," words which belong to one of the five senses. Or words that act and seem to use their muscles, like "flick" or "balance." (2)

In this way, practically working on Shakespeare to arrive at understanding lends itself rather well, I think, to what Adrian Noble (former artistic director of the RSC) calls "a theater of poetry," a form of art that, rooted deeply in its classical origins, would seek to awaken the imagination of its audiences through love and respect for words while satisfying our eternal craving for myths and twice-told tales.

This can only be achieved at some cost. There is indeed a difficult battle to fight and hopefully win "the battle of the word to survive." This phrase was coined by Michael Redgrave at the beginning of the 1950s, a period when theater began to be deeply influenced by more physical forms, such as mime. (3) Although the context is obviously different, the fight today is of the same nature.

LISTENING TO SHAKESPEARE

Because of the influence of television, our way of speaking as well as listening has changed. It is crucial to be aware of this. We can get fairly close to the way *Henry V* or *Hamlet* was staged in Shakespeare's time; we can try also to reconstruct the way English was spoken. But somehow, all these fall short of the real and most important goal: the Elizabethan ear. How did one "hear" a Shakespeare play? This is hardest to know. My personal view is that we will probably never know for sure. We are, even when we hear a Shakespeare play or a recording from the past, bound irrevocably to modernity. The Elizabethan ear was no doubt different from our own, as people were not spoken to or entertained in the same way. A modern voice has to engage us in a different way in order to make us truly listen in a society that seems to rely solely on the belief that image is truth, that it is more important to show than to tell.

Sometimes, we say that a speech in Shakespeare, or even an entire production, is not well-spoken, not up to standard. What do we mean by that? Evidently, there are a certain number of "guidelines" that any actor now has to know when working on a classical text. Yet, even when these are known, actors still have to make choices when they speak. A sound is not a sound without somebody to lend an ear to it: rhetoric is nothing without an audience.

There are a certain number of factors that affect the receiver's ear. These can be cultural factors such as the transition between different acting styles or the level of training that our contemporary ear has had. There are also personal and emotional factors. Often we feel the performance was not well-spoken because, somehow, it did not live up to our expectations of how we think it should have been performed. Is it that many of us have a self-conscious model, perhaps our own first experience of Shakespeare, that meant something to us and became our reference point for the future (some treasured performance kept under glass)? Nothing from then on can quite compare with that experience.

Most of the time, however, it is more complex than nostalgia. Take, for example, the thorny area of accent. I remind myself constantly that audibility is not embedded in Received Pronunciation or Standard American. The familiarity that those in power have with speech and the articulate confidence gained from coming from the right quarters can lead us all to hear certain types of voices as outshining others. But, to my mind, the role of theater is at least to question these assumptions so that we do not perpetuate those givens but work towards a broader tolerance.

In Canada on a production of *Twelfth Night*, I was working with an actor who was from Newfoundland. His own natural rhythms in speaking seemed completely at home with Shakespeare's. Is this because his root voice has direct links back to the voice of Shakespeare's time? It does seem that compared to British dialects, which are predominantly about pitch, many North American dialects have a wonderful respect and vibrancy in their use of vowels. Shakespeare's language seems to me very vowel-aware. How useful it is for an actor to isolate the vowels in the spoken words to hear the music they produce, the rich patterns, their direct connection to feelings. North Americans more easily respond to this and allow it to feed their speaking. I can only assume it is closer to how the Elizabethans spoke.

In *Othello* the very names of the characters have a direct connection to one vowel in particular. All the male names, except the Duke, end in the sound OH: Othello, Cassio, Iago, Brabantio, etc. Furthermore, the sound OH ripples through the play both consciously and unconsciously. "Oh" occurs repeatedly and, more interestingly, is contained within other words: "so," "soul," and "know." These words resonate throughout the play, reinforcing another level of meaning. The repeating of the same sounds affects us beyond what we can quite say.

Vowels come from deep within us, from our very core. We speak vowels before we speak consonants. They seem to reveal the feelings that require the consonants to give the shape to what we perceive as making sense.

Working with actors who are bilingual (or ones for whom English is not the native language) is fascinating because of the way it allows the actor to have an awareness of the cadence in Shakespeare. There seems to be an objective perception to the musical patterns in the text, and the use of alliteration and assonance are often more easily heard not just as literary devices, but also as means by which meaning is formed and revealed to an audience.

Every speech pattern (e.g., accent, rhythm) is capable of audibility. Each has its own music, each can become an accent when juxtaposed against another. The point at which a speech pattern becomes audible is in the dynamic of the physical making of those sounds. The speaker must have the desire to get through to a listener and must be confident that every speech pattern has a right to be heard.

SPEAKING SHAKESPEARE

So, the way to speak Shakespeare is not intrinsically tied to a particular sound; rather, it is how a speaker energetically connects to that language. Central to this is how we relate to the form of Shakespeare. Shakespeare employs verse, prose, and rhetorical devices to communicate meaning. For example, in *Romeo and Juliet*, the use of contrasts helps us to quantify Juliet's feelings: "And learn me how to lose a winning match," "Whiter than new snow upon a raven's back." These extreme opposites, "lose" and "winning," "new snow" and "raven's back," are her means to express and make sense of her feelings.

On a more personal note, I am often reminded how much, as an individual, I owe to Shakespeare's spoken word. The rather quiet and inarticulate schoolboy I once was found in the speaking and the acting of those words a means to quench his thirst for expression.

NOTES:

(1) Peter Brook, *The Empty Space* (Harmondsworth: Penguin, 1972)

(2) Ted Hughes, *Winter Pollen* (London: Faber and Faber, 1995)

(3) Michael Redgrave, *The Actor's Ways and Means*
    (London: Heinemann, 1951)

In the Age of Shakespeare

Thomas Garvey

One of the earliest published pictures of Shakespeare's birthplace, from an original watercolor by Phoebe Dighton (1834)

The works of William Shakespeare have won the love of millions since he first set pen to paper some four hundred years ago, but at first blush, his plays can seem difficult to understand, even willfully obscure. There are so many strange words: not fancy, exactly, but often only half-familiar. And the very fabric of the language seems to spring from a world of forgotten assumptions, a vast network of beliefs and superstitions that have long been dispelled from the modern mind.

In fact, when "Gulielmus filius Johannes Shakespeare" (Latin for "William, son of John Shakespeare") was baptized in Stratford-on-Avon in 1564, English itself was only just settling into its current form; no dictionary had yet been written, and Shakespeare coined hundreds of words himself. Astronomy and medicine were entangled with astrology and the occult arts; democracy was waiting to be reborn; and even educated people believed in witches and fairies, and that the sun revolved around the Earth. Yet somehow Shakespeare still speaks to us today, in a voice as fresh and direct as the day his lines were first spoken, and to better understand both their artistic depth and enduring power, we must first understand something of his age.

REVOLUTION AND RELIGION

Shakespeare was born into a nation on the verge of global power, yet torn by religious strife. Henry VIII, the much-married father of Elizabeth I, had

From *The Book of Martyrs* (1563), this woodcut shows the Archbishop of Canterbury being burned at the stake in March 1556

Map of London ca. 1625

defied the Pope by proclaiming a new national church, with himself as its head. After Henry's death, however, his daughter Mary reinstituted Catholicism via a murderous nationwide campaign, going so far as to burn the Archbishop of Canterbury at the stake. But after a mere five years, the childless Mary also died, and when her half-sister Elizabeth was crowned, she declared the Church of England again triumphant.

In the wake of so many religious reversals, it is impossible to know which form of faith lay closest to the English heart, and at first, Elizabeth was content with mere outward deference to the Anglican Church. Once the Pope hinted her assassination would not be a mortal sin, however, the suppression of Catholicism grew more savage, and many Catholics— including some known in Stratford—were hunted down and executed, which meant being hanged, disemboweled, and carved into quarters. Many scholars suspect that Shakespeare himself was raised a Catholic (his father's testament of faith was found hidden in his childhood home). We can speculate about the impact this religious tumult may have had on his plays. Indeed, while explicit Catholic themes, such as the description of Purgatory in *Hamlet*, are rare, the larger themes of disguise and double allegiance are prominent across the canon. Prince Hal offers false friendship to Falstaff in the histories, the heroines of the comedies are forced to disguise themselves as men, and the action of the tragedies is driven by double-dealing villains. "I am not what I am," Iago tells us (and himself) in *Othello*, summing up in a single stroke what may have been Shakespeare's formative social and spiritual experience.

If religious conflict rippled beneath the body politic like some ominous undertow, on its surface the tide of English power was clearly on the rise. The defeat of the Spanish Armada in 1588 had established Britain as a global power; by 1595 Sir Walter Raleigh had founded the colony of Virginia (named for the Virgin Queen), and discovered a new crop, tobacco, which would inspire a burgeoning international trade. After decades of strife and the threat of invasion, England enjoyed a welcome stability. As the national coffers grew, so did London; over the course of Elizabeth's reign, the city would nearly double in size to a population of some 200,000.

Hornbook from Shakespeare's lifetime

A 1639 engraving of a scene from a royal state visit of Marie de Medici depicts London's packed, closely crowded half-timbered houses.

FROM COUNTRY TO COURT

The urban boom brought a new dimension to British life—the mentality of the metropolis. By contrast, in Stratford-on-Avon, the rhythms of the rural world still held sway. Educated in the local grammar school, Shakespeare was taught to read and write by a schoolmaster called an "abecedarian", and as he grew older, he was introduced to logic, rhetoric, and Latin. Like most schoolboys of his time, he was familiar with Roman mythology and may have learned a little Greek, perhaps by translating passages of the New Testament. Thus while he never attended a university, Shakespeare could confidently refer in his plays to myths and legends that today we associate with the highly educated.

Beyond the classroom, however, he was immersed in the life of the countryside, and his writing all but revels in its flora and fauna, from the wounded deer of *As You Like It* to the herbs and flowers which Ophelia scatters in *Hamlet*. Pagan rituals abounded in the rural villages of Shakespeare's day, where residents danced around maypoles in spring, performed "mummers' plays" in winter, and recited rhymes year-round to ward off witches and fairies.

The custom most pertinent to Shakespeare's art was the medieval "mystery play," in which moral allegories were enacted in country homes and village squares by troupes of traveling actors. These strolling players—usually four men and two boys who played the women's roles—often lightened the moralizing with bawdy interludes in a mix of high and low feeling, which would become a defining feature of Shakespeare's art. Occasionally even a professional troupe, such as Lord Strange's Men, or the Queen's Men, would arrive in town, perhaps coming straight to Shakespeare's door (his father was the town's bailiff) for permission to perform.

Rarely, however, did such troupes stray far from their base in London, the nation's rapidly expanding capital and cultural center. The city itself had existed since the time of the Romans (who built the original London Bridge), but it was not until the Renaissance that its population spilled beyond its ancient walls and began to grow along (and across) the Thames, by whose banks the Tudors had built their glorious palaces. It was these two contradictory worlds—a modern metropolis cheek-by-jowl with a medieval court—that provided the two very different audiences who applauded Shakespeare's plays.

Londoners both high and low craved distraction. Elizabeth's court constantly celebrated her reign with dazzling pageants and performances that required a local pool of professional actors and musicians. Beyond the graceful landscape of the royal parks, however, the general populace was packed into little more than a square mile of cramped and crooked streets where theatrical entertainment was frowned upon as compromising public morals.

Just outside the jurisdiction of the city fathers, however, across the twenty arches of London Bridge on the south bank of the Thames, lay the wilder district of "Southwark." A grim reminder of royal power lay at the end of the bridge—the decapitated heads of traitors stared down from pikes at passersby. Once beyond their baleful gaze, people found the amusements they desired, and their growing numbers meant a market suddenly existed for daily entertainment. Bear-baiting and cockfighting flourished, along with taverns, brothels, and even the new institution of the theater.

Southwark, as depicted in Hollar's long view of London (1647). Blackfriars is on the top right and the labels of Bear-Baiting and The Globe were inadvertently reversed.

THE ADVENT OF THE THEATRE

The first building in England designed for the performance of plays—called, straightforwardly enough, "The Theatre"—was built in London when Shakespeare was still a boy. It was owned by James Burbage, father of Richard Burbage, who would become Shakespeare's lead actor in the acting company The Lord Chamberlain's Men. "The Theatre," consciously or unconsciously, resembled the yards in which traveling players had long plied their trade—it was an open-air polygon, with three tiers of galleries surrounding a canopied stage in a flat central yard, which was ideal for the athletic competitions the building also hosted. The innovative arena must have found an appreciative audience, for it was soon joined by the Curtain, and then the Rose, which was the first theater to rise in Southwark among the brothels, bars, and bear-baiting pits.

Even as these new venues were being built, a revolution in the drama itself was taking place. Just as Renaissance artists turned to classical models for inspiration, so English writers looked to Roman verse as a prototype for the new national drama. "Blank verse," or iambic pentameter (that is, a poetic line with five alternating stressed and unstressed syllables), was an adaptation of Latin forms, and first appeared in England in a translation of Virgil's *Aeneid*. Blank verse was first spoken on stage in 1561, in the now-forgotten *Gorboduc*, but it was not until the brilliant Christopher Marlowe (born the same year as Shakespeare) transformed it into the "mighty line" of such plays as *Tamburlaine* (1587) that the power and flexibility of the form made it the baseline of English drama.

Marlowe—who, unlike Shakespeare, had attended college—led the "university wits," a clique of hard-living free thinkers who in between all manner of exploits managed to define a new form of theater. The dates of Shakespeare's arrival in London are unknown—we have no record of him in Stratford after 1585—but by the early 1590s he had already absorbed the essence of Marlowe's invention, and begun producing astonishing innovations of his own.

While the "university wits" had worked with myth and fantasy, however, Shakespeare turned to a grand new theme, English history—penning the three-part saga of *Henry VI* in or around 1590. The trilogy was such a success that Shakespeare became the envy of his circle—one unhappy competitor, Robert Greene, even complained in 1592 of "an upstart crow...beautified with our feathers...[who is] in his own conceit the only Shake-scene in a country."

Such jibes perhaps only confirmed Shakespeare's estimation of himself, for he began to apply his mastery of blank verse in all directions, succeeding at tragedy (*Titus Andronicus*), farce (*The Comedy of Errors*), and romantic comedy (*The Two Gentlemen of Verona*). He drew his plots from everywhere: existing poems, romances, folk tales, even other plays. In fact a number of Shakespeare's dramas (*Hamlet* included) may be revisions of earlier texts owned by his troupe. Since copyright laws did not exist, acting companies usually kept their texts close to their chests, only allowing publication when a play was no longer popular, or, conversely, when a play was *so* popular (as with *Romeo and Juliet*) that unauthorized versions had already been printed.

Demand for new plays and performance venues steadily increased. Soon, new theaters (the Hope and the Swan) joined the Rose in Southwark, followed shortly by the legendary Globe, which opened in 1600. (After some trouble with their lease, Shakespeare's acting troupe, the Lord

pendeſt on ſo meane a ſtay. Baſe minded men all three
of you, if by my miſerie you be not warnd: for vnto none
of you (like mee) ſought thoſe burres to cleaue : thoſe
Puppets (I meane) that ſpake from our mouths, thoſe
Anticks garniſht in our colours. Is it not ſtrange, that
I, to whom they all haue beene beholding: is it not like
that you, to whome they all haue beene beholding, ſhall
(were yee in that caſe as I am now) bee both at once of
them forſaken? Yes truſt them not: for there is an vp-
ſtart Crow, beautified with our feathers, that with his
Tygers hart wrapt in a Players hyde, ſuppoſes he is as
well able to bombaſt out a blanke verſe as the beſt of
you: and beeing an abſolute Iohannes fac totum, is in
his owne conceit the onely Shake-ſcene in a countrey.
O that I might intreat your rare wits to be imploied in
more profitable courſes: & let thoſe Apes imitate your
paſt excellence, and neuer more acquaint them with
your admired inuentions. I knowe the beſt huſband of

Greene's insult, lines 9–14

Chamberlain's Men, had disassembled "The Theatre" and transported its timbers across the Thames, using them as the structure for the Globe.) Shakespeare was a shareholder in this new venture, with its motto "All the world's a stage," and continued to write and perform for it as well. Full-length plays were now being presented every afternoon but Sunday, and the public appetite for new material seemed endless.

The only curb on the public's hunger for theater was its fear of the plague—for popular belief held the disease was easily spread in crowds. Even worse, the infection was completely beyond the powers of Elizabethan medicine, which held that health derived from four "humors" or internal fluids identified as bile, phlegm, blood, and choler. Such articles of faith, however, were utterly ineffective against a genuine health crisis, and in times of plague, the authorities' panicked response was to shut down any venue where large crowds might congregate. The theaters would be closed for lengthy periods in 1593, 1597, and 1603, during which times Shakespeare was forced to play at court, tour the provinces, or, as many scholars believe, write what would become his famous cycle of sonnets.

The Next Stage

Between these catastrophic closings, the theater thrived as the great medium of its day; it functioned as film, television, and radio combined as well as a venue for music and dance (all performances, even tragedies, ended with a dance). Moreover, the theater was the place to see and be seen; for a penny

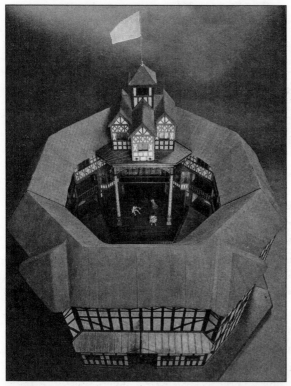

Famous scale model of The Globe completed by Dr. John Cranford Adams in 1954. Collectively, 25,000 pieces were used in constructing the replica. Dr. Adams used walnut to imitate the timber of the Globe, plaster was placed with a spoon and medicine dropper, and 6,500 tiny "bricks" measured by pencil eraser strips were individually placed on the model.

you could stand through a performance in the yard, a penny more bought you a seat in the galleries, while yet another purchased you a cushion. The wealthy, the poor, the royal, and the common all gathered at the Globe, and Shakespeare designed his plays—with their action, humor, and highly refined poetry—not only to satisfy their divergent tastes but also to respond to their differing points of view. In the crucible of Elizabethan theater, the various classes could briefly see themselves as others saw them, and drama could genuinely show "the age and body of the time his form and pressure," to quote Hamlet himself.

In order to accommodate his expanding art, the simplicity of the Elizabethan stage had developed a startling flexibility. The canopied platform of the Globe had a trap in its floor for sudden disappearances, while an alcove at the rear, between the pillars supporting its roof, allowed for "discoveries" and interior space. Above, a balcony made possible the love scene in *Romeo and Juliet*; while still higher, the thatched roof could double as a tower or rampart. And though the stage was largely free of scenery, the costumes were sumptuous—a theater troupe's clothing was its greatest asset. Patrons were used to real drums banging in battle scenes and real cannons firing overhead (in fact, a misfire would one day set the Globe aflame).

With the death of Elizabeth, and the accession of James I to the throne in 1603, Shakespeare only saw his power and influence grow. James, who considered himself an intellectual and something of a scholar, took over the patronage of the Lord Chamberlain's Men, renaming them the King's Men; the troupe even marched in his celebratory entrance to London. At this pinnacle of both artistic power and prestige, Shakespeare composed *Othello*, *King Lear*, and *Macbeth* in quick succession, and soon the King's Men acquired a new, indoor theater in London, which allowed the integration of more music and spectacle into his work. At this wildly popular venue, Shakespeare developed a new form of drama that scholars have dubbed "the romance," which combined elements of comedy and tragedy in a magnificent vision that would culminate in the playwright's last masterpiece, *The Tempest*. Not long after this final innovation, Shakespeare retired to Stratford a wealthy and prominent gentleman.

BEYOND THE ELIZABETHAN UNIVERSE

This is how Shakespeare fit into his age. But how did he transcend it? The answer lies in the plays themselves. For even as we see in the surface of his drama the belief system of England in the sixteenth century, Shakespeare himself is always questioning his own culture, holding its ideas up to the light and shaking them, sometimes hard. In the case of the Elizabethan faith in astrology, Shakespeare had his villain Edmund sneer, "We make guilty of our disasters the sun, the moon, and stars; as if we were villains on necessity." When pondering the medieval code of chivalry, Falstaff decides, "The better part of valor is discretion." The divine right of kings is questioned in *Richard II*, and the inferior status of women—a belief that survived even the crowning of Elizabeth—appears ridiculous before the brilliant examples of Portia (*The Merchant of Venice*), and Rosalind (*As You Like It*). Perhaps it is through this constant shifting of perspective, this relentless sense of exploration, that the playwright somehow outlived the limits of his own period, and became, in the words of his rival Ben Jonson, "not just for an age, but for all time."

track 48

Conclusion of the Sourcebooks Shakespeare Julius Caesar
Derek Jacobi

About the Online Teaching Resources

The Sourcebooks Shakespeare is committed to supporting students and educators in the study of Shakespeare. A website with additional articles and essays, extended audio, a forum for discussions, and other resources can be found (starting in August 2006) at www.sourcebooksshakespeare.com. To illustrate how the Sourcebooks Shakespeare may be used in your class, Jeremy Ehrlich, the head of education at the Folger Shakespeare Library, contributed an essay called "Working with Audio in the Classroom." The following is an excerpt:

One possible way of approaching basic audio work in the classroom is shown in the handout [on the site]. It is meant to give some guidance for the first-time user of audio in the classroom. I would urge you to adapt this to the particular circumstances and interests of your own students.

To use it, divide the students into four groups. Assign each group one of the four technical elements of audio—volume, pitch, pace, and pause—to follow as you play them an audio clip or clips. In the first section, have them record what they hear: the range they encounter in the clip and the places where their element changes. In the second section, have them suggest words for the tone of the passage based in part on their answers to the first. Sections three and four deal with tools of the actor. Modern acting theory finds the actor's objective is his single most important acting choice; an actor may then choose from a variety of tactics in order to achieve that objective. Thus, if a character's objective on stage is to get sympathy from his scene partner, he may start out by complaining, then shift to another tactic (asking for sympathy directly? throwing a tantrum?) if the first tactic fails. Asking your students to try to explain what they think a character is trying to get, and how she is trying to do it, is a way for them to follow this process through closely. Finally, the handout asks students to think about the meaning (theme) of the passage, concluding with a traditional and important tool of text analysis.

As you can see, this activity is more interesting and, probably, easier for students when it's used with multiple versions of the same piece of text. While defining an actor's motivation is difficult in a vacuum, doing so in relation to another performance may be easier: one Othello may be more concerned with gaining respect, while another Othello may be more concerned with obtaining love, for instance. This activity may be done outside of a group setting, although for students doing this work for the first time I suggest group work so they will be able to share answers on some potentially thought-provoking questions . . .

For the complete essay, please visit www.sourcebooksshakespeare.com.

Acknowledgments

The series editors wish to give heartfelt thanks to the advisory editors on *Julius Caesar*, David Bevington and Peter Holland, whose brilliance, keen judgment, and timely advice were irreplaceable during the process of assembling this book.

We are incredibly grateful to the community of Shakespeare scholars for their generosity in sharing their talents, collections, and even their address books. We would not have been able to together such an august list of contributors without their help. First, a sincere thanks to our text editor and *Julius Caesar* scholar, Rob Ormsby, not just for his impeccable work, but also for being a pleasure to work with. Thanks as well to Tom Garvey, Doug Lanier, Jeffrey Horowitz, and Andrew Wade for their marvelous essays. Extra appreciation goes to Doug Lanier for all his guidance and the use of his personal Shakespeare collection. Jeremy Ehrlich's fantastic essay is a cornerstone of our website; we are so grateful for his work. We want to acknowledge the editors of our other editions who have contributed much to the series: Terri Bourus and William Williams. We are grateful to William for his continuing guidance on textual issues, though any errors in this edition are ours.

We want to single out Tanya Gough, the proprietor of The Poor Yorick Shakespeare Catalog, for all her efforts on behalf of the series. She was an early supporter, providing encouragement from the very beginning and jumping in with whatever we needed. For her encyclopedic knowledge of Shakespeare on film and audio, for introducing us into her estimable network, and for a myriad of other contributions too numerous to mention, we offer our deepest gratitude.

Our research was aided immensely by the wonderful staff at Shakespeare archives and libraries around the world: Jane Edmonds and Ellen Charendoff from the Stratford Festival Archives; David Way, Richard Fairman, and the Sound Archives group from the British Library; Susan Brock and the staff at The Shakespeare Birthplace Trust; Georgianna Ziegler, Richard Kuhta, Jeremy Ehrlich, and everyone at the Folger Shakespeare Library; Lynne Farrington from the Annenberg Rare Book & Manuscript Library at the University of Pennsylvania; and Gene Rinkel, Bruce Swann, Nuala Koetter, and Madeline Gibson, from the Rare Books and Special Collections Library at the University of Illinois. These individuals were instrumental in helping us gather audio: Carly Wilford, Justyn Baker, Janet Benson, Susan Loewenberg, Linn Lancett-Miles, and Daniela Suleiman. We appreciate all your help.

From the world of drama, the following shared their passion with us and helped us develop the series into a true partnership between between the artistic and academic communities. We are indebted to: Bonnie J. Monte, Bridget Daley, and the team at the Shakespeare Theatre of New Jersey, Drew Cortese, Joe Plummer, Marilyn Halperin and the team at Chicago Shakespeare Theater, Michael Kahn, Catherine Weidner, Liza Holtmeier, Lauren Beyea, and the team at The Shakespeare Theatre Company, Jeffrey Horowitz and Arin Arbus from Theater for a New Audience, Amy Richard and the team at the Oregon Shakespeare Festival, George Joseph, Michal Daniel, Gerry Goodstein, the 2005 *Julius Caesar* cast from the Shakespeare Theatre of New Jersey, and Nancy Becker of The Shakespeare Society.

With respect to the audio, we are extremely grateful to the excellent work of Catherine Weidner, who answered a last-minute call for help with the narration script. We extend our heartfelt thanks to our narrating team: our director, John Tydeman, our esteemed narrator, Sir Derek Jacobi, and the staff of Motivation Studios. John has been a wonderful, generous resource to us and we look forward to future collaborations. We owe a debt of gratitude to Nicolas Soames for introducing us and for being unfailingly helpful. Thanks also to the "Speaking Shakespeare" team: Andrew Wade, Drew Cortese, and Lyron Bennett for that wonderful recording.

Our personal thanks for their kindness and unstinting support go to our friends and our extended families.

Finally, thanks to everyone at Sourcebooks who contributed their talents in realizing The Sourcebooks Shakespeare—in particular, Samantha Raue, Todd Stocke, Megan Dempster, and Katie Fetter.

Audio Credits

In all cases, we have attempted to provide archival audio in its original form. While we have tried to achieve the best possible quality on the archival audio, some audio quality is the result of source limitations. Archival audio research by Marie Macaisa. Narration script by Catherine Weidner and Marie Macaisa. Audio editing by Motivation Sound Studios, Marie Macaisa, and Todd Stocke. Narration recording, audio engineering, and mastering by Motivation Sound Studios, London, UK. Recording for "Speaking Shakespeare" by Sotti Records, New York City, USA.

Photo Credits

Every effort has been made to correctly attribute all the materials reproduced in this book. If any errors have been made, we will be happy to correct them in future editions.

Photos from the Shakespeare Theatre of New Jersey's 2005 production directed by Brian B. Crowe and the Theater for a New Audience's 2003 production directed by Karin Coonrod are copyright © 2006 Gerry Goodstein. Photos are credited on the pages in which they appear.

Photos from the Public Theater's 2000 production directed by Barry Edelstein are copyright © 2006 Michal Daniel. Photos are credited on the pages in which they appear.

Photos from the Shakespeare Theatre Company's 1993–94 production directed by Joe Dowling are copyright © 2006 Richard Anderson. Photos are credited on the pages in which they appear.

Photos and images from the May 28, 1957 staging of the Royal Shakespeare Company at the Shakespeare Memorial Theatre directed by Glen Byam Shaw are courtesy of the Rare Book and Special Collections Library, University of Illinois at Urbana-Champaign. Photos are credited on the pages in which they appear.

Photos from the 1953 movie directed by Joseph Mankiewicz are copyright © 2006 John Springer Collection/Sunset Boulevard/CORBIS. Photos are credited on the pages in which they appear.

Photos from the Royal Shakespeare Company's 1972 production directed by Trevor Nunn are copyright © 2006 Royal Shakespeare Company. Photos are credited on the pages in which they appear.

Photos from the Public Theater's 1979 production directed by Michael Langham, the 1962 production directed by Joseph Papp, and the 1987–88 production directed by Stuart Vaughan are copyright © 2006 George E. Joseph. Photos are credited on the pages in which they appear.

Photos from the 2005 production at the Barbican Theatre, London directed by Deborah Warner are copyright © 2006 Robbie Jack/CORBIS. Photos are credited on the pages in which they appear.

Photos from the 1937–38 production directed by Orson Welles are copyright © 2006 CORBIS. Photos are credited on the pages in which they appear.

Photos from the 1970 movie directed by Stuart Burge are courtesy of Douglas Lanier. Photos are credited on the pages in which they appear.

Photo of George Coulouris in "In Production: *Julius Caesar* through the Years" courtesy of the Billy Rose Theatre Collection, The New York Public library for the Performing Arts, Astor, Lenox and Tilden Foundations.

William Shakespeare signature (on the title page) and images from "In Production: *Julius Caesar* through the Years" courtesy of Mary Evans Picture Library.

Images from "In the Age of Shakespeare" courtesy of The Folger Shakespeare Library.

Postcard photos from the early 20th century are courtesy of Harry Rusche. Photos are credited on the pages in which they appear.

About the Contributors

Text Editor

Robert Ormsby received his PhD from the University of Toronto in 2005. Besides essays on Canadian performances of classical drama (*Toronto Slavic Quarterly*, May 2003; *Shakespeare Bulletin*, Summer 2004), his publications include Descriptive Entries of Folger Library collection prompt-books for *Coriolanus* productions by John Philip Kemble, Samuel Phelps, and Henry Irving (*The Shakespeare Collection*) and a review of Shakespeare and the Force of Modern Performance by W.B. Worthen (*Renaissance Quarterly*, Summer 2004).

Series Editors

Marie Macaisa spent twenty years in her first career: high tech. She has a BS in computer science from the Massachusetts Institute of Technology and a MS in artificial intelligence from the University of Pennsylvania. She edited the first two books in the series, *Romeo and Juliet* and *Othello*, contributed the "Cast Speaks" essays, and is currently at work on the next set.

Dominique Raccah is the founder, president, and publisher of Sourcebooks. Born in Paris, France, she has a bachelor's degree in psychology and a master's in quantitative psychology from the University of Illinois. She also serves as series editor of *Poetry Speaks* and *Poetry Speaks to Children*.

Advisory Board

David Bevington is the Phyllis Fay Horton Distinguished Service Professor in the Humanities at the University of Chicago. A renowned text scholar, he has edited several Shakespeare editions including the *Bantam Shakespeare* in individual paperback volumes, *The Complete Works of Shakespeare* (Longman, 2003), and *Troilus and Cressida* (Arden, 1998). He teaches courses in Shakespeare, Renaissance Drama, and Medieval Drama.

Peter Holland is the McMeel Family Chair in Shakespeare Studies at the University of Notre Dame. One of the central figures in performance-oriented Shakespeare criticism, he has also edited many Shakespeare plays, including

A Midsummer Night's Dream for the Oxford Shakespeare series. He is also general editor of Shakespeare Survey and co-general editor (with Stanley Wells) of Oxford Shakespeare Topics. Currently he is completing a book on *Shakespeare on Film* and editing Coriolanus for the Arden 3rd series.

ESSAYISTS

Thomas Garvey has been acting, directing, or writing about Shakespeare for over two decades. A graduate of the Massachusetts Institute of Technology, he studied acting and directing with the MIT Shakespeare Ensemble, where he played Hamlet, Jacques, Iago, and other roles, and directed *All's Well That Ends Well* and *Twelfth Night*. He has since directed and designed several other Shakespearean productions, as well as works by Chekhov, Ibsen, Sophocles, Beckett, Moliere, and Shaw. Mr. Garvey currently writes on theatre for the *Boston Globe* and other publications.

Jeffrey Horowitz is the founder and artistic director of Theatre for a New Audience (TFANA) in New York City. Founded in 1979, TFANA's mission is to help develop and vitalize the performance and study of Shakespeare and classic drama. TFANA's productions and artists have been recognized with many awards and nominations, including the Lortel, Drama Desk, Drama League, OBIE, and Tony. In 2001, TFANA became the first US theatre to be invited to bring a production of Shakespeare to the Royal Shakespeare Company (RSC). TFANA toured *Cymbeline* (directed by Bartlett Sher) to Stratford-upon-Avon, and in 2007, their *Merchant of Venice* featuring F. Murray Abraham will be featured as part of the RSC's Complete Works festival.

Douglas Lanier is an associate professor of English at the University of New Hampshire. He has written many essays on Shakespeare in popular culture, including "Shakescorp Noir" in *Shakespeare Quarterly* 53.2 (Summer 2002) and "Shakespeare on the Record" in *The Blackwell Companion to Shakespeare in Performance* (edited by Barbara Hodgdon and William Worthen, Blackwell, 2005). His book *Shakespeare and Modern Popular Culture* (Oxford University Press) was published in 2002. He's currently working on a book-length study of cultural stratification in early modern British theater.

Andrew Wade was head of voice for the Royal Shakespeare Company from 1990 to 2003 and voice assistant director from 1987 to 1990. During this time he worked on 170 productions and with more than 80 directors. Along with Cicely Berry, Andrew recorded *Working Shakespeare* and the DVD series on *Voice and Shakespeare,* and he was the verse consultant for the movie *Shakespeare In Love.* In 2000, he won a Bronze Award from the New York International Radio Festival for the series *Lifespan,* which he co-directed and devised. He works widely teaching, lecturing and coaching throughout the world.